Ronald Fairbairn

T0323875

In this concise and introductory book, David P. Celani examines the work of Ronald Fairbairn, one of the pioneers of Object Relations Theory.

Ronald Fairbairn: A Contemporary Introduction adopts a unique approach to Fairbairn's work and legacy. Organizing the book thematically, Celani makes connections between Fairbairn's disparate and often convoluted papers, offering the reader a more accessible insight into the work of this eminent analyst. He looks in turn at Fairbairn's field-defining work on Object Relations, split consciousness, repression and the impact of parental neglect on a child's developing personality. Celani also explores Fairbairn's assessment of infants' dependency on their maternal figure and brings his ideas into the 21st century. Considering the work of Philip Bromberg in tandem with that of Fairbairn, Celani considers the practical, clinical and theoretical implications of Fairbairn's model.

This volume is essential reading for analysts in practice and training interested in the work of Fairbairn and the impact Object Relations have had on psychoanalysis as a whole.

David P. Celani is a retired psychologist and adjunct professor at the Object Relations Institute in New York City, USA.

Routledge Introductions to Contemporary Psychoanalysis

Aner Govrin, Ph.D.
Series Editor
Yael Peri Herzovich, Ph.D.
Executive Editor

"Routledge Introductions to Contemporary Psychoanalysis" is one of the prominent psychoanalytic publishing ventures of our day.

The series' aim is to become an encyclopedic enterprise of psychoanalysis, with each entry given its own book.

This comprehensive series is designed to illuminate the intricate landscape of psychoanalytic theory and practice. In this collection of concise yet illuminating volumes, we delve into the influential figures, groundbreaking concepts, and transformative theories that shape the contemporary psychoanalytic landscape.

At the heart of each volume lies a commitment to clarity, accessibility, and depth. Our expert authors, renowned scholars and practitioners in their respective fields guide readers through the complexities of psychoanalytic thought with precision and enthusiasm. Whether you are a seasoned psychoanalyst, a student eager to explore the field, or a curious reader seeking insight into the human psyche, our series offers a wealth of knowledge and insight.

Each volume serves as a gateway into a specific aspect of psychoanalytic theory and practice. From the pioneering works of Sigmund Freud to the innovative contributions of modern theorists such as Antonino Ferro and Michal Eigen, our series covers a diverse range of topics, including seminal figures, key concepts, and emerging trends. Whether you are interested in classical psychoanalysis, object relations theory, or the intersection of neuroscience and psychoanalysis, you will find a wealth of resources within our collection.

One of the hallmarks of our series is its interdisciplinary approach. While rooted in psychoanalytic theory, our volumes draw upon insights from psychology, philosophy, sociology, and other disciplines to offer a holistic understanding of the human mind and its complexities.

Each volume in the series is crafted with the reader in mind, balancing scholarly rigor with engaging prose. Whether you are embarking on your journey into psychoanalysis or seeking to deepen your understanding of specific topics, our series provides a clear and comprehensive roadmap.

Moreover, our series is committed to fostering dialogue and debate within the psychoanalytic community. Each volume invites readers to critically engage with the material, encouraging reflection, discussion, and further exploration.

We invite you to join us on this journey of discovery as we explore the ever-evolving landscape of psychoanalysis.

ראש הטופס
Aner Govrin – Editor

Otto Kernberg
A Contemporary Introduction
Frank Yeomans, Diana Diamond, Eve Caligor

Erich Fromm
A Contemporary Introduction
Sandra Buechler

Narcissism
A Contemporary Introduction
Richard Wood

The Death Drive
A Contemporary Introduction
Rossella Valdrè

Depression
A Contemporary Introduction
Marianne Leuzinger-Bohleber

Ronald Fairbairn
A Contemporary Introduction
David P. Celani

Ronald Fairbairn

A Contemporary Introduction

David P. Celani

Routledge
Taylor & Francis Group

LONDON AND NEW YORK

Designed cover image: © Michal Heiman, Asylum 1855–2020,
The Sleeper (video, psychoanalytic sofa and Plate 34),
exhibition view, Herzliya Museum of Contemporary Art, 2017

First published 2025
by Routledge
4 Park Square, Milton Park, Abingdon, Oxon OX14 4RN

and by Routledge
605 Third Avenue, New York, NY 10158

*Routledge is an imprint of the Taylor & Francis Group, an
informa business*

© 2025 David P. Celani

British Library Cataloguing-in-Publication Data
A catalogue record for this book is available from the British Library

ISBN: 978-1-032-49515-6 (hbk)
ISBN: 978-1-032-49348-0 (pbk)
ISBN: 978-1-003-39418-1 (ebk)

DOI: 10.4324/9781003394181

Typeset in Times New Roman
by Apex CoVantage, LLC

Contents

Introduction

W.R.D. Fairbairn proposed his structural model in 1944 as part of his revision of classical metapsychology, but his concepts were largely ignored by his analytic colleagues until the emergence of the relational perspective in the 1980s. Fairbairn viewed the defense of dissociation as the key to understanding the human psyche and reduced the role that repression played. The dissociative defense in Fairbairn's model is the fundamental way in which the infant/toddler protects himself/herself from memories of traumatic empathic failures on the part of his/her parents. These failures, if consciously remembered, would rupture the child's essential attachment to his/her needed object. The attachment between infant and mother was seen as the fundamental motivation of the infant in Fairbairn's view, and he boldly replaced libido theory with "attachment theory", a shift that alienated the analytic community. Fairbairn then redefined the source of the human unconscious from an inherited package of drives to the dissociated memories of traumatic parental failures that could not be processed by the child's under-developed ego structure. This too alienated the analytic community, as Freud's instinctual unconscious was seen as the basic psychic building block that could not be modified or eliminated. Fairbairn also presented a model of human consciousness that was composed of multiple and shifting ego states, which were contained in the individual's inner world and were isolated from each other as well as from the conscious central ego. He also recognized that the rejected child became powerfully attached to bad object parent(s) who had abused/neglected him because the cumulative trauma that was contained in his unconscious ego states retarded normal emotional development and prevented the child from differentiating from his objects. Additionally, he observed that the split-off and isolated part-selves held in the

DOI: 10.4324/9781003394181-1

individual's unconscious prevented integration of the good and bad aspects of external objects. He saw that the two fundamental developmental processes, differentiation and integration, were both impeded by the parents' failures of empathy and support during development, thus placing his theory in the category of a modern "arrested development" model. These once-radical concepts, which were overwhelmingly rejected by the analytic community of his day, are currently mainstream and part of the body of psychoanalytic knowledge, and can be seen in newer relational models, yet despite this there are few citations of Fairbairn's specific work.

This is my fifth text focused on the work of W.R.D. Fairbairn, and as in the past, I feel that there is more to be said about this remarkable analytic theorist and his prescient psychoanalytic model. Fairbairn played a major role in my own development as I emerged as a clinical psychologist in 1974 with some familiarity with analytic theory and a "standard" degree in clinical psychology. However, I was completely unprepared to deal with my first group of patients, in that three of my initial six patients showed clear evidence of dissociation. In my work with them, I could see these individuals suddenly shift their views of their parents from being critical to another completely different and opposite view – one of adoration – during our sessions. I was vaguely familiar with multiple ego states, but did not know the psychological reasons for their existence. Each of my first six patients also startled me by the fact that they were slavishly attached to brutally rejecting families, either by continuing to live with them or returning to the families home every weekend. To me, this return to hostile, indifferent and caustic parents seemed illogical, yet when I questioned my patients about their return to their families, they defended their self-destructive attachments fiercely.

Over time I became familiar with splitting (without even knowing the term) to the point that I named the libidinal ego (I had not heard of Fairbairn's model at that time) as "hope springs eternal". This sub-ego appeared in many sessions, signaled by a sudden shift of the patient's focus from an examination of their often-difficult developmental histories to a completely defensive and idealized view of their parents. This would often occur when we were speaking about their history of childhood neglect or abuse. The eruption of this new ego state ceased to surprise me after experiencing it again and again. I concluded that our focused discussion of the many parental failures that my patients had actually experienced had overwhelmed their capacity to accept the reality of their childhood histories. By the time that Mitchell and

Greenberg's book "Object Relations in Psychoanalytic Theory" was published in 1983, I had been in practice for eight years, and by then I was ready for a model that directly addressed "attachment to bad objects", splitting and " a multiplicity of egos". After reading the section on Fairbairn, I discovered that without ever knowing it, I had been immersed in the same type of patient population that Fairbairn was writing about in the 1940s. I found reading his text *Psychoanalytic Studies of the Personality* (1952) to be an enormous relief. My focus was on Fairbairn's descriptions of patient pathology and his structural model, part of which my patients had inadvertently introduced me to back in 1975. Since that time I have read and reread Fairbairn many times and have become far more critical of the many errors in his model, which I will point out in this text. However, after removing his many misstatements and logical errors, his model addresses the factors that require the child to split his objects, and paradoxically binds him/her to the very people who damaged and subverted his/her emotional development. The intention of this book is to present the reader with a clear, well-reasoned and most importantly eminently usable and practical version of Fairbairn's model which can be employed as a primary model in the clinical setting without recourse to other models of psychoanalysis.

Fairbairn is not generally accepted by analytic clinicians who have used classical metaphors because his model contradicts so many of the fundamental assumptions of Freud. One of the most basic differences between the two models is that Fairbairn's model is absolutely committed to seeing the human personality as a two-person system with the individual's self as always being involved in an internal or external relationship with another individual, as noted in the following passage from Mitchell:

In this vision the basic unit of study is not the individual as a separate entity whose desires clash with an external reality, but an interactional field within the individual arises and struggles to make contact and to articulate himself. *Desire* is experienced always *in the context of relatedness*, and it is that context which defines its meaning. Mind is composed of relational configurations. The person is comprehensible only within this tapestry of relationships, past and present. Analytic inquiry entails participation in, and observation, uncovering, and transformation of these relationships and their internal representations.

(Mitchell, 1988:3)

This book differs from the four previous books I have written based on his model in that I have included two previously unmentioned sources of inspiration that influenced Fairbairn's thinking, one religious and the second one, the prior work of Ian Suttie, who wrote a prototype of much of Fairbairn's model in regard to the child's absolute dependency on his objects. Finally, this text relies on many other more recent sources from current object relations writers compared to my previous work. This new focus demonstrates how Fairbairn's ideas have continued to influence the field of psychoanalysis.

In my practice, I viewed the analytic models that I had read from a practical point of view metaphorically, as a "toolbox" that helped me focus on problem areas that were important in diagnosis and in treatment. As I will suggest, Fairbairn's model, as originally presented, is strong on psychopathology and diagnosis, and less helpful when it comes to treatment. The "toolbox" approach to using a model has a certain ruthlessness to it in that there is no excusing or working around parts of a model that either make no sense or are patently incorrect.

The book begins with an explanation of the reasons for Fairbairn's model obscurity, including its radical elimination of drive theory, which alienated the analytic community. Fairbairn's model had other problems, including the fact that it was unfinished, used mixed metaphors and finally lacked illustrations of how to apply his structural model in clinical applications. Then the chapter examines Fairbairn's early life, including his decision to leave his clerical studies and pursue psychoanalysis. It then describes the sources of ideas that Fairbairn drew upon, including religious teaching, philosophy and the work of Ian Suttie, a contemporary Scottish psychiatrist whose book, "The Origins of Love and Hate" (1935) was owned and heavily underlined by Fairbairn (Clarke, 2011) and is quoted extensively.

Then the chapter reviews his writing on the child's absolute dependency on his objects for life, comfort, safety and protection. Fairbairn described the impact of early parental empathy as key to the developing child's mental health, as traumatic incidents of parental empathic failure had to be dissociated by the child and forced into his/her unconscious. The dissociated memories populate the child's unconscious with independent realities that are too toxic for him or her to remember and compromise the functioning of the central ego. The most important insight in this chapter is Fairbairn's realization that the rejected/neglected child is more rather than less attached to his objects, as he is "fixated" on his maternal object, waiting for the necessary emotional supplies that would help him differentiate and move into life.

The second chapter begins with the impact of Fairbairn's work on the current literature of trauma with passages from recent authors, including Blizard (2019), Davies (1998) and Gumley and Liotti (2019), which demonstrate that Fairbairn's fundamental concepts are still being discussed and written about today. This is followed by Fairbairn's unique description of the schizoid personality disorder, with a significant update by Bromberg (1998) again illustrating the viability of Fairbairn's ideas. This is followed by Fairbairn's identification of "substitutive satisfactions" (currently video games) to which the child turns to avoid the harsh interpersonal family environment. Rehberger (2014)'s work is then quoted, which introduces in no uncertain terms the startling brutality of the environment in which many children live, and which eventuates in the schizoid defense. The discussion turns to Fairbairn's writing on differentiation from the object which is impeded by lack of empathic care. The next section describes Fairbairn's new definition of the unconscious, one of his many revolutionary challenges to classical metapsychology. Fairbairn redefined the unconscious as being composed of dissociated interpersonal events which were too traumatic for the child to remember consciously, thus also placing his model as an early trauma/dissociation model. Fairbairn, in one of his most clear, complete and elegant definitions of psychopathology ever written, describes the three factors that, if present in the child's environment during the developmental years, create psychopathology. Fairbairn then described the power of internalized objects and how the dissociated sub structures impact the developing character of the child. The chapter ends with a discussion of Fairbairn's "Moral Defense of Bad Objects".

Chapter Three is the longest and covers the nature of trauma, dissociation and the process of splitting. Interestingly, Bromberg (1998) cites the positive benefits from dissociation (which is usually *only* seen as a serious emotional handicap), because it allows the central ego to continue to function, despite the fact that there are now small independent sub egos with their own "truths" that populate the individual's unconscious. Fairbairn's thought processes that led up to the construction of his six-part structural model are then described, with a focus on the mostly unconscious, split-off pairs of self and objects, which are the key to understanding his model. Perhaps the greatest insight in this chapter is that the combination of allure followed by rejection keeps the child attached to the: "bad object". The intense emotional relationship between the two members of each pair of structures are described: the first pair comprises the intimidated, needy and simultaneously enraged antilibidinal ego (the child's memory of himself when being neglected or abused) with its desire to reform the abusing/neglecting rejecting object. The second part-self and part-object pair comprises the libidinal ego, which sees a completely different aspect of the same object (called the exciting object), which appears to be a parent suffused with hidden love. The goal of the libidinal ego is to find a way to squeeze love out of the exciting object. This is followed by a discussion of the developmental origins of the central ego and the gradual emergence of a single identity which can vary in strength according to the child's developmental history. A more detailed description of the four mostly unconscious structures follows, along with clinical examples that can be observed in clinical interviews with patients. Finally, there are a number of quotes from authors who are completely unconnected with psychoanalysis but have discovered Fairbairn's part-self or part-object structures in their own personalities. These writers serve to support the reality that these structures exist in the external world.

Chapter Four begins with the necessary modifications that have to be made to Fairbairn's model in order to use it as a "master narrative" in the clinical setting. Fairbairn made numerous errors in his model, including disallowing the internalization of the good object and misidentifying the mechanism that triggered the dominant sub-ego structure to be repressed and replaced by another structure. He also misunderstood the nature of the relationship between the antilibidinal ego and its rejecting object partner, as well as the relationship of the two pairs of structures to each other in the unconscious. *Simply put, his model is not a functional tool that can be used with patients as he presented it without the changes outlined in this chapter*. The next discussion is of the three completely distinct sources of resistance in Fairbairn's model, which emerge directly from his model of trauma and dissociation. His description of the resistances that the clinician will face is as clear and well reasoned as any part of his model. Fairbairn's goals of treatment are also discussed, the most important of which is to gradually introduce the central ego to the split-off, dissociated material that was once too toxic for it to process. The chapter ends with Mitchell's quote describing the active seeking out of pathological partners by the patient so his unconscious internal structures can find someone who is willing to reenact his/her early pathological patterns.

Chapter Five begins with an illustration of how to use Fairbairn's structural model as a diagnostic tool, with a colorful example from Searles (1965). The following section uses Schafer's (1992, 1996) definition of psychoanalysis as a co-created narrative directed by the analyst. The treatment goal when using Fairbairn's metapsychology is to gradually introduce the patient's central ego to the split off parts of the relationship between the child's self and the rejecting object that were once too toxic to experience. The presence of an interested and attentive "other" is essential to the process. This discussion is followed by an example of a clinical narrative, using Fairbairn's concepts. Use of a narrative by the analyst involves allying himself/herself with the patient's central and antilibidinal egos and slowly undermining the patient's beliefs regarding the legitimacy of the rejecting object. This is followed by a quote from Skolnick (2014) that illustrates a patient's extreme rejecting object interaction with him that provoked an equally extreme antilibidinal response by Skolnick. This is followed by three relatively long case examples, with the first illustrating the derepression of powerful and telling metaphors from an abused and neglected woman's unconscious. The second is of a woman who displayed attachment to her bad object family, and her enactment of her powerful sub-egos in a battering relationship with an inappropriate man, whom she sought out because he was able to engage her powerful sub-egos. The book ends with the clinical illustration of a patient who was raised by extremely controlling parents whom she initially respected, despite the fact that they caused severe developmental damage to her and her two siblings. The playful relationship that developed between us in the treatment setting, which made fun of her rigid and bombastic father, allowed her to escape from a trap that her family had set up to prevent her from returning home.

References

Blizard, R. (2019). The role of double blinds, reality testing and chronic relational trauma in the genesis and treatment of borderline personality disorder. In Moskowitz, A., Dorahy, M., and Schafer, I. Eds., *Psychosis, Trauma and Dissociation: Evolving Perspectives on Severe Psychopathology*. Hoboken, NJ: John Wiley & Sons, pp. 367–380.

Bromberg, P. (1998). *Standing in the Spaces*. New York: Psychology Press.

Clarke, G. (2011). Suttie's influence on Fairbairn's object relations theory. *Journal of the American Psychoanalytic Association*, 59 (5): 939–959.

Davies, J.M. (1998). Repression and dissociation – Freud and Janet: Fairbairn's new model of unconscious process. In Skolnick, N.J. and Scharff, D.E. Eds., *Fairbairn Then and Now*. Hillsdale, NJ: The Analytic Press, pp. 53–69.

Fairbairn, W.R.D. (1944). Endopsychic structure considered in terms of object relationships. In *Psychoanalytic Studies of the Personality*. London: Routledge & Kegan Paul, 1952, pp. 82–132.

Fairbairn, W.R.D. (1952). *Psychoanalytic Studies of the Personality*. London: Routledge & Kegan Paul.

Greenberg, J.R. and Mitchell, S.A. (1983). *Object Relations in Psychoanalytic Theory*. Cambridge, MA: Harvard University Press.

Gumley, A. and Liotti, G. (2019). An attachment perspective on Schizophrenia. In Moskowitz, A., Dorahy, M., and Schafer, Eds., *Psychosis, Trauma and Dissociation: Evolving Perspectives on Severe Psychopathology*. Hoboken, NJ: John Wiley & Sons, pp. 97–116.

Mitchell, S. (1988). *Relational Concepts In Psychoanalysis: An Integration*. Cambridge, MA: Harvard University Press.

Rehberger, R. (2014). Viewing Camus's *The Stranger* from the perspective of W.R.D. Fairbairn's object relations. In Clarke, G. and Scharff, D. Eds., *Fairbairn and the Object Relations Tradition*. London: Karnac Books, pp. 461–470.

Schafer, R. (1992). *Retelling a Life: Narration and Dialogue in Psychoanalysis*. New York: Basic Books.

Schafer, R. (1996). Authority, evidence, and knowledge in the psychoanalytic relationship. In Renick, O. Ed., *Knowledge and Authority in the Psychoanalytic Relationship*. Northvale, NJ: Jason Aronson, 1998, pp. 227–244.

Searles, H. (1958). The schizophrenic's vulnerability to the therapist's unconscious processes. In Searles, H.F. Ed., *Collected Papers on Schizophrenia and Related Subjects*. New York: International Universities Press, 1965.

Skolnick, N.J. (2014). The analyst as a good object: A Fairbairnian perspective. In Clarke, G. and Scharff, D.E. Eds., *Fairbairn and the Object Relations Tradition*. London: Karnac, pp. 249–262.

Suttie, I. (1935). *The Origins of Love and Hate*. London: Pelican Books.

Chapter 1

Fairbairn 2024

Greenberg and Mitchell (1983), in their foundational text on the emergence of the relational/structure models of psychoanalysis that evolved from Freud's drive/structure model, began their chapter on Fairbairn with the following quote:

> In a series of dense and fertile papers written during the 1940s, W.R.D. Fairbairn developed a theoretical perspective which, along with Sullivan's "interpersonal psychiatry", provides the purest and clearest expression of the shift from the drive/structure model to the relational/structure model.
>
> (Greenberg and Mitchell, 1983:151)

Today, Fairbairn's model remains virtually unknown (and unused by clinicians) as there has been no support for his model from an institute or journal dedicated to his work, thus leaving his theory undeveloped. Despite the lack of overt acknowledgment of his ideas, his concepts have swept through the field of psychoanalysis and are currently found in trauma-dissociation theories, which incorporate many if not most of his ideas. Fairbairn's model posed an impossible philosophical challenge to the analytic community regarding the essential nature of the human infant when it was written in the 1940s. Classical theory held that the infant is possessed by libidinal and aggressive drives characterized as "demonic" (Grotstein and Rinsley, 1994:9), while Fairbairn viewed the infant as an innocent victim of a traumatic environment which failed to nurture and cherish him, thus impeding his development.

Fairbairn's position lost in this philosophical contest, despite the fact that the fundamental notion that early relational trauma has severe

DOI: 10.4324/9781003394181-2

consequences for the child's developing ego structure is commonplace in the field of psychoanalysis today. There are multiple and overlapping reasons for his model being virtually abandoned by the field of psychoanalysis. The most prominent reason that Fairbairn remains unknown was his uncompromising nature, coupled with a complete lack of understanding of how attached his fellow analysts were to Freud and Freudian theory. Fairbairn had a bold intellect and challenged the entire basis of Freudian metapsychology, alone, as an independent clinician and philosopher in Edinburgh, Scotland. He was isolated and far from London, which was the center of analytic activity in the UK. His model was introduced to the analytic community via a series of papers, each of which was published separately, and then collected in his only text, *Psychoanalytic Studies of the Personality* (1952).

Fairbairn was largely ignored because he offended the psychoanalytic community by replacing Freud's libido theory with the child's need for attachment to the maternal object. Libido theory was the center of Freud's model, and libidinal energy was assumed to power the development of the human psyche. Thus, by eliminating libido Fairbairn was in effect an elimination of Freud. Worse, in his revolutionary paper of 1958, *On the Nature and Aims of Psycho-Analytical Treatment*, Fairbairn further offended his colleagues by boldly saying that his psychoanalytic model replaced the entirety of Freud's metapsychology.

In brief, my theoretical position may be said to be characterized by four main conceptual formulations:-viz. (a) a theory of dynamic psychical structure, (b) a theory to the effect that libidinal activity is inherently and primarily object-seeking, (c), a resulting theory of libidinal development couched, not in terms of presumptive zonal dominance, but in terms of the quality of dependence, and (d) a theory of the personality couched exclusively in terms of internal object relationships. The first two of these formulations taken in combination may be said to represent a substitute for two of Freud's basic theories – his classic libido theory and his final theory of instincts. The third formulation is offered as a revision of Abraham's version of Freud's theory of libidinal development. And finally, my object relations theory of the personality is intended to replace Freud's description of the mental constitution in terms of the id, the ego and the superego.

(Fairbairn, 1958:374)

It would be difficult to conceive of a more ill-timed and alienating quote to be published in 1958 in the *International Journal of Psychoanalysis*, as the field of psychoanalysis was still overwhelmingly dominated by classical Freudian thinkers and practitioners. Fairbairn's uncompromising intellect and profound sense that he was correct led him to believe that his completely different understanding of the very same material that the Freudian model had explained, with its instinctual and energetic metaphors, would be accepted because of its inherent logic. There was no way of finding commonality between the models. As a consequence, members of the analytic community were asked to choose between two very different models of human development and of psychological functioning; no one chose Fairbairn, if indeed they paid any attention to his work at all. Psychoanalysis had only a single "community" and by alienating it, Fairbairn was left with absolutely no one to promote his ideas.

The lack of acceptance of Fairbairn's model was enhanced by a number of other issues that combined to guarantee that he would be ignored in his own time and then soon forgotten. In addition to alienating the analytic community by his dismissal of Freud's libido theory, his bold presentation of his alternative theory to his colleagues was seen as a traitorous act, simply because he was a member of the analytic community. The field of psychoanalysis in Fairbairn's day was condemned by the general public and by the popular press as a theory that undermined society's norms and standards because of the emphasis on childhood sexuality. The analytic community became self-protective as it was the target of constant external criticism. Fairbairn's challenge to the instinctual basis of psychoanalysis was seen by members of the analytic community, already sensitive to criticism, as an attack on them by one of their own members. This was simply intolerable, as classical psychoanalysis was (and is) held dear by many members of the analytic community. Freud and Freudianism is part of their self definition, and Fairbairn's model, with all of its complexity, devoid of instinctual drive and missing the three-part metaphor of the human psyche, was dismissed and not considered to be "real" psychoanalysis.

The next problem that impeded the adoption of Fairbairn's model was his writing style, which is very difficult and frustrating for the student or professional. Much of his writing is akin to stream of consciousness, as opposed to Freud's beautifully crafted essays. In the following passage, Greenberg and Mitchell (1983) describe Fairbairn's writing style as one of the issues that prevented the adoption of his model:

> Although he did pull together his major contributions into a single volume, he did not rework them into a coherent and comprehensive theory, but left them in their original chronological order and form. Consequently, the reader is faced not with a single theory but with a series of different formulations, with varying yet related focuses, circling again and again over the same territory, yet not wholly consistent with each other.
>
> (Greenberg and Mitchell, 1983:153)

The Greenberg and Mitchell quote *minimizes* the problems with Fairbairn's writing. The majority of Fairbairn's papers are dense, speculative and filled with unsupported assumptions and sudden shifts in focus, thus making them exceedingly difficult to follow. To add to the confusion, he uses libidinal metaphors and language freely, as he was trained in one discipline and was simultaneously struggling to give birth to another completely contradictory view of psychoanalysis. Classical analytic language was the only language that existed at the time. His papers articulate every random thought he had as he mused and doubled back from one speculative position to the next, never correcting past errors, but rather pushing forward with a welter of new speculations on nearly every page. Fairbairn's writing is also filled with endless philosophical debates with Freud, and these debates detract from rather than add to his core ideas. His papers are metaphorically similar to an artist's preliminary sketches that lie buried under a painting, but in Fairbairn's case, his preliminary ideas are fully exposed. Fairbairn was somewhat aware of the difficulty of his writing, as in his introduction to his book of collected papers, *Psychoanalytic Studies of the Personality* (1952), he noted the unfinished nature of his model:

> These papers constitute a series: and I feel it is very necessary to draw attention to the fact that this series of papers represent, *not the elaboration of an already established point of view, but the progressive development of a line of thought.*
>
> (Fairbairn, 1952: introduction X)

Despite the fact that Fairbairn understood the unfinished nature of his essays, he greatly underestimated the difficulties that he was presenting to his readers. He assumed that his thought processes were logical and could be followed by the reader – which is simply not the case. Most amazingly, within this confusing tangle of ideas there are, on occasion, beautifully composed clinical observations that are filled with insights that stand out from his normal speculations. These well-composed passages speak directly to the reader, articulating the fundamental principles upon which his model is based, as if all the preliminary static was necessary for him to formulate his finished ideas. The major goal of this text is to present the reader with a clear and well-reasoned version of Fairbairn's basic positions without the rhetorical confusion that has obscured his revolutionary principles of human psychological development for so long.

Another major obstacle in his writing is that Fairbairn never applied his structural model to clinical examples. His structural theory itself was, in addition, filled with logical problems that hampered its applicability. He presented very few examples of his patients in the first place, and never used his structural model to identify patient statements as coming from one structure or the other. Thus, there is no clear application of his theory from which to begin using his structural model. As a result, there are no guidelines for the interested clinician to follow, leaving him/her with a series of well-thought-out observations with no guidance on how to put them to use, other than in a general way. My own writing on Fairbairn (Celani, 1993, 1994, 1999, 2001, 2005, 2007, 2010, 2014a, 2014b, 2016, 2020) has focused from the very beginning on the applicability of his model to diagnosis and to the treatment of major character disorders.

Finally, the last impediment to the adoption of Fairbairn's model, which I see evidence of today, is the fundamental tenet of the relational viewpoint, which is that the self has to be understood as always being in a relationship with either an internal or external object. Thus, in any communication there are always two participants: the self and the object. This results in Fairbairn's six-part (three self and object pairs) structural theory, which is at odds with the classical intrapsychic three-part metaphor of the mind. Freud's metaphor has been established in the field of psychoanalysis as the baseline reality of the human psyche. Fairbairn's insistence of seeing the self as always in a relationship with an object is also contrary *to our way of thinking about ourselves*, as each of us experiences the world from the perspective of a single self, which is "an acquired, developmentally adaptive illusion" (Bromberg, 1998:273). The shift from a one-person psychology to a two-person psychology is still ongoing. In addition, Fairbairn's labeling of the split-off selves and the part objects of his structural model and the manner in which they relate to each other in the unconscious (the antilibidinal ego relates only to its rejecting object partner, and the libidinal ego relates only to its fantasy produced exciting object partner) are strange terms not used by any other model. To add to the confusion, Fairbairn changed the traditional meaning of words used by the analytic community. For instance, in his concept of the libidinal (part) ego, "libidinal" does not mean instinctual drive, but rather a part-self of the child who is desperately seeking love from its object. In teaching Fairbairn, I have also found that these sub-egos are easily confused with each other. Each of the four unconscious structures refer to a part self or a part object, which are also concepts that are at variance with traditional ways of thinking of the self. The sum total of these impediments to the adoption of Fairbairn's model have doomed it to obscurity. Fairbairn was aware of this reality in his lifetime. Despite all of his work, he had few supporters with the exception of friendships with Sutherland and Guntrip, and he also faced hostility in his home life from his wife (for his absences), from his University of Edinburgh colleagues who were suspicious of all of psychoanalysis (Sutherland, 1989:xii), and finally from the analytic community, which saw him as a traitor because of his attacks on classical theory. As a consequence, his work was simply ignored by most in the analytic community, while a few others saw his work as an interesting but fundamentally weak and inconsequential philosophical challenge to Freud, with no inherent value in the clinical office.

His last paper (1963), published in the *International Journal of Psychoanalysis*, is analogous to Luther's 95 theses tacked to the church door, which was used as a community notice board (Grotstein, 1994:175, Celani, 2010:211). Fairbairn's paper was composed of a bare 17 single-sentence assertions – a last protest before his death on December 30th, 1964. Despite this, Scharff and Birtles (1997) note that even with all these problems in his model, his work influenced other seminal British psychoanalytic writers:

His understanding of the importance of the relationship with the mother and family in infant and childhood development came fifteen years before Winnicott's and Bowlby's published accounts and expansion of ideas in this realm, and were an important part of the

climate in which they later developed their contributions. His theory still remains fundamental to a rigorous underpinning of their work.
(1997:1086–1087)

This text is an attempt to liberate Fairbairn's model from its current status as a way-station in the development of the relational perspective to a view of it as a robust, usable model of psychopathology and of psychoanalysis.

Fairbairn's Personal Background and the Influences That Impacted the Development of His Model

Fairbairn was the only child of upper-middle-class parents; his father was a surveyor in Edinburgh and sent his son (as a day student) to the Merchiston Castle School, which was a private school for boys (Sutherland, 1989:4). Sutherland, who was Fairbairn's biographer, notes that his early childhood was dominated by strict parents who relied on religious doctrine as the basis for their philosophy of child rearing:

That her staunchly Presbyterian husband should choose an English Episcopalian as his wife, perhaps represented a latent need on his part to mitigate the harshness of the Calvinist tradition. There was, however, little yielding in this respect, because Cecilia Leefe was strict to the point of being a martinet in bringing her son up to conform to the formalities of their class, religion and otherwise. Fairbairn senior was a friendly man, to those that knew him, fond of entertaining and interested in his society as he saw it. His wife was known amongst their friends as one who maintained a well-ordered establishment with a marked sense of what was "proper".
(Sutherland, 1989:2)

During his childhood, Fairbairn witnessed a traumatic scene involving his father, who had difficulty urinating in public. The following description is from Sutherland (1989:70–71), who was quoting Fairbairn's written memories of the event from when he was eight years old. The family was traveling on the Highland railway, which had no available bathrooms. Fairbairn's father had to urinate, and his mother held up a newspaper to screen the elder Fairbairn from others who were in the same compartment. His father had great difficulty urinating, and this event led Fairbairn to develop "Bashful Kidney", a neurotic symptom that prevented him from using public bathrooms if anyone else was present. This symptom limited his ability to travel as an adult, and it may have impacted his ability to speak directly about his model to the analytic community of his day.

Early Influences on Fairbairn's Conception of the Human Psyche

As a young man, Fairbairn attended Edinburgh University and graduated in 1907 with an honors degree in philosophy. He decided on a career in the church and took courses in Hellenistic studies and theology in Germany. These courses deepened his existing interest in philosophy, and Fairbairn considered himself a philosopher before becoming an analyst, as noted in the following quote from Hoffman & Hoffman:

Fairbairn's philosophy studies at Edinburgh University stoked his spiritual interests in the discipline. Between 1912 and 1914, Fairbairn studied theology at the universities of Kiel, Strasbourg and Manchester. His theological studies included Hellenistic Greek . . . "Hellenistic Greek, also called Koine, or Biblical Greek, is a mainstay of formal theological studies".

(Hoffman and Hoffman, 2014:71)

Scharff and Birtles (2014) also noted that in Germany Fairbairn also studied the works of Hegel, which helped him to see the self as always in an interaction with an external "other" which becomes an active part of self creation.

In the Hegalian philosophical account, the innate capacities for language, symbolization and rational thought are understood to be dependent for their development on an adequate environment. The dialectic exchange between subject and object (the "other") results in a new relationship or synthesis. The relationships between subject and object provide the progressive epistemological element necessary for the growth of language and thought Fairbairns understanding of this philosophical point of view enabled him to place relational meaning and value, rather than gratification, at the motivational center.

(Scharff and Birtles, 2014:8)

After completing three semesters in the German universities, he began studying for the intermediate degree in divinity at the University of London (Sutherland, 1989:8). After graduation, Fairbairn then returned to Edinburgh University at 25 years of age and enrolled for the doctorate in divinity of the Presbyterian Church. His studies were interrupted by WW1, and he signed up in 1915 and served in Egypt (Sutherland, 1989:8).

Another source of Fairbairn's understanding of the human psyche, not surprisingly, came from his studies in divinity. Hoffman and Hoffman (2014) cite a specific and well-known sermon written by Thomas Chalmers, founder of the Free Church of Scotland, in 1855. It addresses the possibility of ridding oneself of a bad object by replacing it with a good object in its stead − a key concept in Fairbairn's approach to treatment.

If the throne which is placed there must have an occupier and the tyrant that now resides has occupied it wrongfully, he may not leave a bosom which would rather retain him than be left in desolation . . . In a word, if the way to disengage the heart from the "love" of one great and ascendant object, is to fasten it in positive love to another, then it is not by exposing the worthlessness of the former, but by addressing to the mental eye the worth and excellence of the latter, that all old things are to be done away and all things are to become new . . . In fullest accordance with the mechanism of the heart, a great moral revolution may be made to take place upon it.

(Hoffman and Hoffman, 2014:82)

This quote was translated loosely into Fairbairn's fundamental understanding of treatment. An individual who has a dependent and loving/hating attachment to a hostile parent, and who fears desolation if he leaves, can transfer his dependency/love to a better and more supportive and loving person, thus allowing his thwarted development to continue. Fairbairn described this approach to treatment in his 1958 paper in the simplest terms; the analyst presents himself as a good (alternative) object, works through the patient's defenses and over time enters the individual's inner world and displaces the bad object.

In November 1916, while serving in the military, Fairbairn experienced a major life-changing event, which was his visit to the Craiglockhart Hospital, where W.H.R. Rivers was treating shell-shocked victims of war traumas.

On 16 November, 1916, while on active duty in the Royal Artillery in Scotland and shortly before his posting to the Middle East, Fairbairn visited the Craiglockhart Hospital. . . . The hysterical injuries, or war neuroses, that he saw there made an indelible impression on him, and he decided to take medical training in order to become a psychotherapist.

(Scharff and Birtles, 2014:7)

After the war, Fairbairn gave up his divinity studies and instead attended medical school and began an analysis with Ernest Connell, originally a successful Australian businessman who came to Edinburgh in 1920 and became a psychoanalyst. Connell saw Fairbairn from July 1921 to December 1922 for three to five sessions a week (Scharff and Birtles, 2014:7). Upon completion of his training, Fairbairn held a number of different positions as noted in the following summary:

Fairbairn started private psychoanalytic practice in 1923 when he qualified in medicine. From that date to 1935 he held a variety of appointments at mental hospitals in and around Edinburgh, which ran concurrently with his lectureships in psychology in the discipline of mental philosophy from 1927–1935, and in psychiatry from 1931–1932. His special subject was adolescence, and he also taught philosophy. He used psychoanalytic techniques in his clinical work at the University Psychological Clinic, and, from 1933, at the Child and Juvenile Clinic.

(Scharff and Birtles, 2014:7)

Another influence on Fairbairn that was more immediate and powerful than philosophy or Calvinist doctrine came from Ian Dichart Suttie, a Scottish psychiatrist born in 1889, the same year as Fairbairn in nearby Glasgow. His book, *The Origins of Love and Hate*, published in 1935, was found in Fairbairn's library by Graham Clarke (2011). It was a heavily underlined copy of the 1939 edition of Suttie's book, which was a wide-ranging critique of Freudian theory, but which did not offer an alternative model. Suttie would likely have been more influential in the field of psychoanalysis had he not died in 1935 on the eve of the publication of his only book.

It is striking to see just how many fundamental premises Fairbairn took from Suttie's work and wove into his own formulations. It is fair to say that Fairbairn's writing on dependency owes a huge debt to Suttie's observations, and that Suttie can be considered one of the founders of object relations theory. Suttie begins by noting the complete dependency of the infant on the mother, and his need for the goodwill and cooperation of his parents for his ongoing development. The following quote from Suttie was adapted by Fairbairn as one of the foundational concepts of his own work, which was soon to appear in his theoretical papers.

> It differs fundamentally from psycho-analysis in introducing the conception of an innate need for companionship which is the infant's only way of self preservation. This need, giving rise to parental and fellowship "love", I put in the place of Freudian Libido, and regard it as generally independent of genital appetite.
>
> (Suttie, 1935:5)

This assertion can be considered as the very outset of the relational revolution, in which Suttie displaced instinctual drive and replaced it with the infant's dependency needs, which he describes as the "innate need for companionship". This statement had an absolute foundational impact on Fairbairn's model of the human psyche. Suttie followed this up with a second statement which differentiates the human infant from newborn animals that have some (nascent) abilities to defend themselves, either by fleeing or striking back, as compared to the completely dependent and helpless human infant.

> It (the infant) is born with a simple attachment-to-mother who is the sole source of food and protection. Instincts of self-preservation such as would be appropriate for an animal which has to fend for itself would be positively destructive to the dependent infant, whose impulses *must* be adapted to its mode of livelihood, namely pseudo parasitism.
>
> (Suttie, 1935:12)

The description of the infant's relationship to its parent as "pseudo parasitism" is unappealing, but it does convey the reality that the child can do absolutely nothing for itself and must rely completely on the protection and goodwill of its mother. Suttie continued to develop this theme in the following passage, where he again confronts classical metapsychology.

> We can reject therefore once and for all the notion of the infant mind being a bundle of cooperating or competing instincts, and suppose instead that it is dominated from the beginning by the need to retain the mother – a need if thwarted must produce the utmost extreme terror and rage, since the loss of the mother is, under natural conditions, but the precursor of death itself. We have now to consider whether this attachment-to-mother is merely the sum of the infantile bodily needs and satisfactions which refer to her, or whether the *need for a mother is primarily presented to the child's mind as a need for company and as a discomfort in isolation.*
>
> (Suttie, 1935:12–13, italics in the original)

This quote is clearly reflected in Fairbairn's writing, with his emphasis on the child's desperate need for attachment to his object. All of Fairbairn's defenses are designed to shield the infant and toddler from knowing, or experiencing, the reality that his mother is the source of his discomfort. Today we substitute "fear of abandonment" for Suttie's term "discomfort in isolation", but the fundamental meaning is the same.

Suttie then addresses perhaps the most basic disagreement between relational theories and classical psychoanalysis, which is the source of rage and anger in the human psyche. The classical model assumes that aggression is part of human instinctual inheritance, whereas Suttie saw it as an extreme attempt to capture the mother's attention with the goal of getting *her to help him/her* reduce fear, pain or distress, which the infant cannot do for himself/herself.

> I am suggesting that in animals born or hatched in a state of nurtural dependency the whole instinct of self preservation, including the potential disposition to react with anger or fear, is at first directed toward the mother. Anger is then aimed, not at the direct removal of frustration or attainment of the goal of the moment, still less at her destruction, but *at inducing the mother to accomplish these wishes for the child.* Instead of being the most desperate effort at *self-help* it has become the most insistent demand upon the *help*

of others – the most empathic plea that cannot be overlooked. It is now the maximal effort to *attract* attention, and as such must be regarded as a protest against unloving conduct rather than as aiming at destruction of the mother, which would have fatal repercussions upon the self. Hatred, I consider, is just a standing reproach to the hated person, and owes all its meaning to a demand for love.

(Suttie, 1935:18)

This is a powerful challenge to the classical assertion that rage is inherent in the biological inheritance of all human beings. Suttie sees it differently, defining rage as a demand for help that only turns to rage when the object is indifferent or unresponsive. In addition, Suttie recognized that the response from the mother determined the infant's sense of safety. A parent who did not comprehend the infant's demand, or was upset and incapable of responding, only increased the infant's anxiety.

As in the case of anger, the response expected and desired is not an identical emotion on the part of the mother. Either anger or apprehension on her part increases the corresponding disturbance in the child's mind. When the child is afraid it is reassured by her confidence and serenity, but not by her indifference and neglect, which is perhaps the worst of all for the child.

(Suttie, 1935:19)

This fundamental position on the source of aggression in the human child creates a complete break with instinct theory, which insists that rage is born within each individual as a simple consequence of being a human. This relational view is far more hopeful and places love at the center of the relationship between mother and infant. In the next quote, Suttie reaffirms the child's attempts to get the mother to help him and to protect him from isolation and abandonment.

I consider then that love of mother is primal in so far as it is the *first formed and directed* emotional relationship. Hate I regard not as a primal independent instinct (see later) but as a development or intensification of separation anxiety, which in turn is *roused* by a threat against love. It is the maximal ultimate appeal in the child's power – the most difficult for the adult to ignore. Its purpose is not death-seeking or death-dealing, but the preservation of the

self from isolation, which is death, and the restoration of a love
relationship.

(Suttie, 1935:25)

Suttie's position on the source of aggression in the infant is both absolutely clear and well-reasoned. Once again, this quote reads like it
came from Fairbairn himself, thus strengthening the hypothesis that
Fairbairn used many of Suttie's positions as the foundation for his
model. It is also possible that Fairbairn had similar ideas himself, but
it appears that Fairbairn took Suttie's well-articulated positions and
placed them into the core of his model. Fairbairn repeatedly emphasizes the child's absolute dependency on his object and his total inability to do anything for himself, thus elevating the importance of a
reassuring and comforting object.

In the next passage, Suttie addresses one of the ways that the child
can comfort himself in the absence of a good-enough mother. He sees
fantasy as a pathway for the infant or child to use in order to feel safe,
even though his current environment is harsh and unyielding.

> But hate of a loved object (ambivalence), as I have said, is intoler-
> able: the love relationship must be preserved as a matter of life or
> death, and there are various means of doing this. . . . An alterna-
> tive is to abandon the mother *as she now appears in reality* for
> the mother as she once appeared and as she is remembered. This
> involves the technique of *taking refuge from reality in fantasy* to
> which reference has already been made.

(Suttie, 1935:34–35)

The substitution of fantasy for reality protects the child when the external environment is harsh and rejecting. Fairbairn expanded Suttie's
concept of the use of fantasy in his description of the development of
his structural theory, specifically in the creation of the libidinal ego
(1944), which promised the deprived and desperate child that love was
just around the corner. This part-ego structure allows the child to live
in a world filled with hope and anticipation, a world in which his/her
essential attachment to the mother survives, despite the reality that the
child lives in a harsh interpersonal environment devoid of love and
support.

Suttie then touched on the process of differentiation as the infant
got older and began to relate to the parent in a more mature manner.

Suttie notes that differentiation can only occur if the child or young adult is convinced that his source of support is dependable and will continue if needed. This is another point that Fairbairn incorporated in his model, saying that the child must be "convinced" that his parents genuinely love him as a person in order to take steps toward differentiation.

> We could say that Christian teachings are concerned with the actual process of socialization-namely the transition from an *exclusive rapport with the parent to an all-embracing rapport with fellows*. Pursuing this analogy (or homology) between the religious needs of the adult and the love needs of the child, we recognize that the condition of renouncing exclusive rapport with the parent is the *assurance of security*. That is, we must be convinced that the parent is "provident" even without continuous solicitation. . . . Even more, we must be assured of our acceptability to the parent: that is to say we must be able to expunge the sense of guilt (original sin). Once we feel sure of "our base of supplies" (of encouragement and of love) we can adventure into fellowship.
>
> (italics in the original, Suttie, 1935:126)

Suttie then added another defense as a way of keeping the mother "all good" in addition to the use of fantasy. The infant and toddler have to defend against recognizing any "badness" in his maternal object because that realization would break the "all good" fantasy that allowed his dependency bond with her to continue. Fairbairn transformed Suttie's idea that the child made himself "all bad" into his "Moral Defense Against Bad Objects", which was his first defense.

> The *Preservation* of the lovableness of the mother. "Mother is good and kind: if she does not love me that is because I am bad. From this starting point is developed what is called by some people "inferiority complex". The ultimate extreme is "melancholia" where the patient has a sense of utter unworthiness.
>
> (Suttie, 1935:35)

Fairbairn's "Moral Defense Against Bad Objects" is a precursor of his latter structural theory. Fairbairn saw children who blamed themselves for the abuse they received at home while working in the orphanage attached to the Edinburgh Hospital (1927–1935), where he had a part-time appointment. Suttie did not explain the underlying mechanism for this psychological defense, which Fairbairn recognized as a primitive type of splitting where the child makes himself bad, thus making the objects around him all good.

Suttie also observed that the child not only needs to be loved by his mother, but also needs his love for his mother accepted and welcomed. This too is an integral part of Fairbairn's model, clearly adopted from Suttie's writings. The two following passages illustrate Suttie's position.

> The anxious sense of separation seems to the infant as much a *rejection of its own gifts* as a refusal of the mother to give. The rejection of the child's "gifts", like any failure to make an adequate response, leads to a sense of badness, unloveable-ness in the self, with melancholia as its culminating expression.
>
> (Suttie, 1935:40)

> The mother-child relationship however (to the child's mind) is a true "balanced" symbiosis: and the *need to give* is as vital therefore, as *the need to get*. The feeling that our gifts (love) are not acceptable is as intolerable as the feeling that "others' gifts are not attainable.
>
> (Suttie, 1935:43)

These observations by Suttie became the bedrock of Fairbairn's writing on the child's dependency on "bad" ungiving objects, and they are additionally important as the foundational concepts of object relations theory.

Fairbairn's Writing on the Child's Absolute Dependency on His Objects

W.R.D. Fairbairn was not a linear writer, and his insights on the infant's and child's vulnerability to empathic failures by his caretakers are present in all six of his significant theoretical papers (1940, 1941, 1943, 1944, 1954, 1958). In the past, I have reviewed his model chronologically (Celani, 1993, 2010), which in hindsight reduces the impact of the totality of his observations as they are scattered throughout these six papers. When grouped together, they offer the reader a clear understanding of the depth of his insights into the vagaries of human development. He has proven to be one of the most sensitive and articulate psychoanalytic theorists in regard to his understanding of the emotional damage done to infants and children who had experienced either abuse or neglect.

A separate difficulty with a chronological presentation of Fairbairn's writing on dependency in his model was that his first theoretical paper (1940) began not with the infant, but rather with his description of adult patients who he defined as "the schizoid", a diagnosis that he himself created. Fairbairn's schizoid patient was not equivalent to the preexisting definition of schizoid patients in the psychiatric or psychoanalytic literature, thus adding additional confusion. Fairbairn described the schizoid as an individual who has "splits" in his ego structure and who created an inner reality through which he was able to avoid his harsh external reality. Then he began to work backward, speculating as to the causes of the adult psychopathology that he saw in this group.

His analytic model is based on his (and Suttie's) observation that infants and children are absolutely and categorically dependent on their maternal objects to provide them with a sense of comfort and safety. When love and support are abundantly present in the infant's and child's environment, these two factors give the child enough reassurance and courage to allow him to slowly differentiate and explore the world beyond his maternal object. When they are absent, differentiation is severely impeded. Fairbairn's clearest statement on the child's absolute dependency on his objects appears in his 1941 paper.

The outstanding feature of infantile dependence is its unconditional character. The infant is completely dependent upon his object not only for his existence and physical well-being, but also for the satisfaction of his psychological needs. . . . By contrast, (to the adult) the very helplessness of the child is sufficient to render him dependent in an unconditional sense . . . He has no alternative but to accept or reject his object-an alternative that is liable to present itself to him as a choice between life and death. Dependency is exhibited in its most extreme form in the intra-uterine state: and we may legitimately infer that, on its psychological side, this state is characterized by an absolute degree of identification and absence of differentiation. Identification must thus be regarded as representing the persistence into extra-uterine life of a relationship existing before birth. In so far as identification persists after birth, the individual's object constitutes not only his only world, but also himself.

(Fairbairn, 1941:47)

This quote demonstrates that Fairbairn was thinking about dependency and lack of differentiation as the infant's mode of experiencing the world at the very outset of life. At this early stage the infant's self is a potential that is about to emerge. Thus the object is the whole world to the infant and the quality of care that he/she receives will determine the development of his/her particular self over the course of his differentiation, and later the ability to integrate disparate views of his objects. The extreme dependency of the infant coexists with extreme vulnerability to failures of empathic caretaking. Thus, severe and/or repeated parental lapses of empathy and caring are experienced as abandonment, which is felt by the infant or child as a complete loss of self (which is yet unformed), as well as the loss of the entire world around him. This extreme sense of danger of annihilation forces the infant or child to use the defense of dissociation, as abandonment at this early stage of life is experienced as the ultimate trauma and has to be obliterated from the child's awareness.

As you read Fairbairn, you can sense his struggle to articulate a model which was formed around the issue of dependency as he put down similar ideas repeatedly in his early papers. Thus, many of the quotes I will cite have similar characteristics and tone as Fairbairn was working over his ideas on the consequences to the infant of parental emotional failure. One of the formative experiences of Fairbairn's professional life, which was previously noted, was his part-time appointment as one of the supervisors of the orphanage attached to the Royal Edinburgh Hospital from 1927–1935. He observed children that were taken from their homes and inquired about their relationships with their parents. He also noticed how desperately they wanted to return to the very homes in which they had been abused, which formed his later concept of "attachment to bad objects".

The following passage from his 1940 paper elaborates upon the "early oral attitude" that eventuated from early experiences of not being loved by his mother. At this time, Fairbairn mistakenly believed that internalization was a defensive process and not an automatic way of experiencing the world, and that only frustrating objects were internalized. Note that in this quote he uses the term "bad object" for the first time, without defining it.

> The early oral attitude is one characterized, not only by taking, but also by incorporating or internalizing. Regressive reinstatement of the early oral attitude would appear to be most readily brought about by a situation of emotional frustration in which the child comes to feel (a) that he is not really loved for himself as a person by his mother, and (b) that his own love for his mother was not really valued and accepted by her. This is a highly traumatic situation giving rise to a further situation characterized as follows:
>
> (a) The child comes to regard his mother as a bad object in so far as she does not seem to love him.
> (b) The child comes to regard outward expressions of his own love as bad, with the result that, in an attempt to keep his love as good as possible, he tends to keep his love inside himself.
> (c) The child comes to feel that love relationships with external objects in general are bad, or at least precarious. The net result is that the child tends to transfer his relationships with his objects into the realm of inner reality.
>
> (1940:17–18)

This quote covers many of Fairbairn's (and Suttie's) fundamental themes. The first is that lack of love from the parent was traumatic and has consequences that are taken into his developing personality and enacted later in life. He also echoes Suttie's position that the rejection of the child's love toward his mother is another painful source of emotional abandonment.

Fairbairn had concluded very early in his writing that there was an ineluctable connection between early emotional deprivation and developmental retardation. This causal relationship was one of the foundations of his theory. The following passage is a fragment of a longer quote in which Fairbairn was describing the development of the schizoid personality. Here the focus is on maternal failure to support the child, which hinders further differentiation from her. Without maternal support and encouragement, the child is unwilling to risk leaving the source of his already tenuous emotional nourishment, for fear that external reality is too frightening to cope with as he/she is completely lacking in support.

> That early in life they gained the conviction, whether through apparent indifference or through apparent possessiveness on the part of their mother, that their own mother did not really love and value them as a person in their own right, and that influenced by a resultant sense of deprivation and inferiority, they remained profoundly fixated upon their mother.
>
> (1940:23)

Most adults find it surprising and counter-intuitive that the rejected infant clings to his maternal object *more tightly* than does the emotionally supported infant. Fairbairn cites deprivation and inferiority as the reason that the child clings, but did not mention the fear factor. Separation from the mother produces fear when the child is unsure of his maternal object's availability in the first place; thus the act of leaving her is very risky, as he is leaving his (imperfect) source of emotional supplies. The unsupported infant has not been given enough reassurance for him to begin to separate from the very parent who is depriving him, and to whom he clings. Thus he is not able to explore the external world and begin the development of his own ego structure. Instead he becomes more and more focused on the parent, waiting for the support and reassurance that would allow him to separate.

The following quote from his 1941 paper is a more elaborate and well-thought-out version of the child's need for emotional support for him to differentiate from his object, and it is a clear example of the Greenberg and Mitchell (1983) observation that Fairbairn circled around the same issues repeatedly. He again states that the fundamental consequence to the child who had experienced a consistent lack of love from his maternal object is that his/her efforts to differentiate from her are completely thwarted.

> What emerges as clearly as anything else from the analysis of such a case is that the greatest need of a child is to obtain conclusive assurance (a) that he is genuinely loved as a person by his parents, and (b) that his parents genuinely accept his love. It is only insofar as such assurance is forthcoming in a form sufficiently convincing to enable him to depend safely upon his real objects that he is able to gradually renounce infantile dependence without misgiving. In

the absence of such assurance his relationship with his objects is fraught with too much *anxiety over separation* to enable him to renounce the attitude of infantile dependence; for such a renunciation would be equivalent in his eyes to forfeiting all hope of ever obtaining the satisfaction of his unsatisfied emotional needs. Frustration of his desire to be loved as a person and have his love accepted is the greatest trauma that a child can experience.

(Fairbairn, 1941:39–40)

This beautifully written passage demonstrates that Fairbairn saw psychopathology as a result of repeated failures of the relational environment due to parental neglect that collectively prevented emotional growth and gradual differentiation from the object. He was convinced that the deprivation of love was the key to understanding the child's thwarted or delayed emotional development. The child's only defense against experiencing or re-experiencing parental indifference or lack of empathy is to use the dissociative defense. This defense eliminates the child's sense of emotional dread, which is an exceedingly disruptive emotion that is too threatening for him to integrate into his awareness. The dissociation of intolerable interpersonal rejections into isolated split-off memories also dissociates parts of the central ego (the part central ego that originally experienced the rejecting events). As development proceeds in families lacking empathy for their children, more and more of the child's original central ego is dissociated and lost to the unconscious, thus strengthening the unconscious structures at the expense of the central ego.

As mentioned, Fairbairn worked over his ideas on the impact of parental failures on the developing psyche of the child, and they appear in all of his theoretical papers. He recognized that the child with rejecting parents is placed in an impossible situation. He is utterly dependent as his experience of chronic emotional deprivation makes him increasingly dependent over time as he gets older and fails to differentiate. He/she discovers that it is a dangerous "procedure" (Fairbairn's word) to complain about the treatment that he/she is receiving to the parents who are depriving him/her. The following quotes come from his 1944 paper on structuralization of the unconscious, and it's interesting to note that Fairbairn was still working over the many ramifications of early rejection on the child's emotional needs at this relatively late period of theory creation. The following two passages demonstrate Fairbairn's occasional ability to articulate clinical insights in a beautifully clear, incisive and impactful manner. These quotes also bring to mind the concept of the "double bind" theory of schizophrenia popular in the 1950s.

It is natural for the child, not only to be impulsive, but also to express his feelings on no uncertain terms. Moreover, it is through the expression of his feelings that he makes his chief impression upon his objects. Once ambivalence has been established, however, the expression of feelings toward his mother involves him in a position which must seem to him singularly precarious. Here it must be pointed out that what presents itself to him from a strictly cognitive standpoint as *frustration* at the hands of his mother presents itself to him in a very different light from a strictly affective standpoint. From the latter standpoint, what the child experiences is a sense of lack of love, and indeed emotional *rejection* on his mother's part. This being so, the expression of hate toward her as a rejecting object becomes a very dangerous procedure. On the one hand, it is calculated to make her reject him all the more, and thus increase her "badness" and make her seem *more real* in her capacity as a bad object. On the other hand, it is calculated to make her love him less, and thus to decrease her "goodness" and make her seem *less real* in her capacity of a good object.

(Fairbairn, 1944:112–113)

Fairbairn recognized that the child caught in the grip of a rejecting family had nowhere to go with his distress. To complain to his parents about the way he was being treated would, in all probability, get him into yet another round of increased rejection, and would make his objects seem even more unloving than they already were. The other dilemma for the child is what to do with his love for his parents, who have been indifferent to him in the past. This was Suttie's point: when the child's gifts to the parent are rejected, he is demeaned in terms that his gift of love is of no importance.

At the same time, it also becomes a dangerous procedure for the child to express his libidinal need, i.e. his nascent love, of his mother in the face of rejection at her hands: for it is equivalent to discharging his libido in an emotional vacuum. Such a discharge is accompanied by an affective experience which is singularly devastating. In the older child this experience is one of intense humiliation over the depreciation of his love, which seems to be involved. At a somewhat deeper level (or at an earlier stage) the experience is one of shame over the display of needs which are disregarded or belittled. In virtue of these experiences of humiliation and shame he feels reduced to a state of worthlessness, destitution or beggardom. His sense of his own value is threatened; and he feels bad in the sense of "inferior".

(Fairbairn, 1944:113)

These two quotes demonstrate that Fairbairn really was a master of describing the crushing emotional experience of a child who was living in an unloving environment. The child is blocked in terms of his need for love and support, and equally blocked from demonstrating his love for his parents. Fairbairn's language is powerful, if not thunderous, as he attempts to describe the lasting impact of an unloving family on the child's self-esteem: "He feels reduced to a state of worthlessness, destitution or beggardom".

Bromberg (1998) describes, in more detail than Fairbairn did, just how the parents shape and "create" their child's personality by projecting and affirming aspects that may or may not be present, and ignoring aspects that are present but that they do not like. The child may be completely misunderstood, but because of his dependency, his incomplete central ego and loyalty to his parents' vision of him, he is unable to protest for fear of increased censure. He describes this process that happens over thousands of interactions to the point that the child loses sight of parts of himself due to his parents' disconfirmations.

That is, a parent's primary power to shape a child's sense of self isn't through saying (in words) "you are such and such" (though this certainly does take place) but through relating to the child as though he is already "such and such" and ignoring other aspects of his being as though they don't exist. These "disconfirmed" . . . domains of self remain cognitively unsymbolized as "me" because they have no relational context of meaning to give them life. A child's sense of self thus becomes bonded to the early object through his identity being shaped by who the object both perceives him to be and denies him to be.

(Bromberg, 1998:313)

Bromberg's work, along with others', has kept Fairbairn's foundational notions alive in the world of Object Relations Theory, and his work will be mentioned frequently in the following chapters.

References

Bromberg, P. (1998). *Standing in the Spaces*. New York: Psychology Press.

Celani, D.P. (1993). *The Treatment of the Borderline Patient: Applying Fairbairn's Object Relations Theory in the Clinical Setting*. Madison, CT: International Universities Press.

Celani, D.P. (1994). *The Illusion of Love: Why the Battered Woman Returns to Her Abuser*. New York: Columbia University Press.

Celani, D.P. (1999). Applying Fairbairn's object relations theory to the dynamics of the battered woman. *American Journal of Psychotherapy*, 53 (1): 60–73.

Celani, D.P. (2001). Working with Fairbairn's ego structures. *Contemporary Psychoanalysis*, 37: 391–416.

Celani, D.P. (2005). *Leaving Home: How to Separate from Your Difficult Family*. New York: Columbia University Press.

Celani, D.P. (2007). A structural analysis of the obsessional character: A Fairbairnian perspective. *American Journal of Psychoanalysis*, 67 (2): 119–140.

Celani, D.P. (2010). *Fairbairn's Object Relations Theory in the Clinical Setting*. New York: Columbia University Press.

Celani, D.P. (2014a). Revising Fairbairn's structural theory. In Clarke, G. and Scharff, D. Eds., *Fairbairn and the Object Relations Tradition*. London: Karnac Books, pp. 397–409.

Celani, D.P. (2014b). A Fairbairnian structural analysis of the narcissistic personality disorder. *The Psychoanalytic Review*, 101 (3): 385–409.

Celani, D.P. (2016). Fairbairn's theory of change. *The Psychoanalytic Review*, 103 (3): 341–369.

Celani, D.P. (2020). Applying Fairbairn's object relations theory to the psychological development of Anders Breivik. *The Psychoanalytic Review*, 107 (4): 337–366.

Clarke, G. (2011). Sutties influence on Fairbairn's object relations theory. *Journal of the American Psychoanalytic Association*, 59 (5): 939–959.

Fairbairn, W.R.D. (1940). Schizoid factors in the personality. In *Psychoanalytic Studies of the Personality*. London: Routledge & Kegan Paul, 1952, pp. 3–27.

Fairbairn, W.R.D. (1941). A revised psychopathology of the psychoses and psychoneuroses. In *Psychoanalytic Studies of the Personality*. London: Routledge & Kegan Paul, 1952, pp. 28–58.

Fairbairn, W.R.D. (1943). The repression and return of bad objects (with special references to the "war neuroses"). In *Psychoanalytic Studies of the Personality*. London: Routledge & Kegan Paul, 1952, pp. 59–81.

Fairbairn, W.R.D. (1944). Endopsychic structure considered in terms of object relationships. In *Psychoanalytic Studies of the Personality*. London: Routledge & Kegan Paul, 1952, pp. 82–132.

Fairbairn, W.R.D. (1952). *Psychoanalytic Studies of the Personality*. London: Routledge & Kegan Paul.

Fairbairn, W.R.D. (1954). Observations on the nature of hysterical states. *British Journal of Medical Psychology*, 27: 105–125.

Fairbairn, W.R.D. (1958). On the nature and aims of psycho-analytical treatment. *International Journal of Psychoanalysis*, 39: 374–385.

Fairbairn, W.R.D. (1963). Synopsis of an object-relations theory of the personality. *International Journal of Psychoanalysis*, 44: 224–225.

Greenberg, J.R. and Mitchell, S.A. (1983). *Object Relations in Psychoanalytic Theory*. Cambridge, MA: Harvard University Press.

Grotstein J. and Rinsley, D. (1994). *Fairbairn and the Origins of Object Relations*. New York: The Guilford Press.

Hoffman, M. and Hoffman, L. (2014). Religion in the life and work of W.R.D. Fairbairn. In Clarke, G. and Scharff, D. Eds., *Fairbairn and the Object Relations Tradition*. London: Karnac Books, pp. 69–85.

Scharff, D.E. and Birtles, E.F. (1997). From instinct to self: The evolution and implications of W.R.D. Fairbairn's theory of object relations. *International Journal of Psychoanalysis*, 78: 1085–1103.

Scharff, D.E. and Birtles, E.F. (2014). From instinct to self: The evolution and implications of W.R.D. Fairbairn's theory of object relations. In Clarke, G. and Scharff, D. Eds., *Fairbairn and the Object Relations Tradition*. London: Karnac Books, pp. 5–25.

Sutherland, J.D. (1989). *Fairbairn's Journey into the Interior*. London: Free Association Books.

Suttie, I. (1935). *The Origins of Love and Hate*. London: Pelican Books.

Chapter 2

The Schizoid Character, the Process of Differentiation and Fairbairn's Model of the Unconscious

The Schizoid Personality

Fairbairn's first theoretical paper that began his theory building was *Schizoid Factors in the Personality* (1940), in which he described young adults who displayed characteristics that he assumed had come from lack of love early in life. He noted that these patients were all suffering from "splits in their ego", which he had not clearly defined at this time. It wasn't until his 1944 paper, *Endopsychic Structure Considered in Terms of Object Relationships* that he introduced his structural theory that fully explained the splitting process and the schizoid character. In Fairbairn's metapsychology, splitting is the process by which dissociated traumatic memories which could not be accepted by the central ego are forcibly held and isolated in the individual's unconscious.

> Among the various characteristics common to the apparently conglomerate group of individuals who fall under the schizoid category as now envisaged three are of sufficient prominence to deserve special mention. These are (1) an attitude of omnipotence, (2) an attitude of isolation and detachment, and (3) a preoccupation with inner reality. . . . So far as the preoccupation of inner reality is concerned, this is undoubtedly the most important of all schizoid characteristics: and it is nonetheless present whether inner reality be substituted for outer reality, identified with outer reality or superimposed upon outer reality.
>
> (Fairbairn, 1940:6–7)

This is an example of Fairbairn presenting an absolutely key concept of his model long before it was fully formed. The quote describes

DOI: 10.4324/9781003394181-3

projection of the individual's inner reality onto external objects or events, which is the mechanism of transference and enactments. In schizoid patients, the inner templates of human relationships, dissociated and split off from the central ego, become more significant than actual events in the external world, and thus, the deeply split off individual sees the same interpersonal scenarios again and again.

Splitting of the ego was seen by Fairbairn as a key aspect of the schizoid personality, which he characterized as being severely deprived of love in their earliest years, and because of the severity of the deprivation the individual was forced to dissociate memories of parental failures. In the following passage, Fairbairn describes what the schizoid individual faced early on in life:

> If we look still further into the sources of the sense of difference from others which characterizes individuals with a schizoid element in their personality, we find evidence of the following among other features: (1) that early in life they gained the conviction, whether through apparent indifference or through apparent possessiveness on the part of their mother, that their mother did not really love and value them as persons in their own right: (2) that, influenced by a resultant sense of deprivation and inferiority, they remained profoundly fixated upon their mother; (3) that the libidinal attitude accompanying this fixation was one not only characterized by extreme dependence, but also rendered highly self-preservative and narcissistic by anxiety over a situation presented itself as involving a threat to the ego.
>
> (Fairbairn, 1940:23)

This quote emphasizes the damage done to the child's ego structure due to parental indifference or hostility. The schizoid state has been discussed by Bromberg (1998), whose description adds to Fairbairn's original point that the child is seeking shelter from a harsh reality from which he cannot escape by seeking the safety and protection that the schizoid state affords the child.

> What intrigued me was that, apart from its dynamic origins as a mode of escape from certain experiences including, for many individuals, annihilation anxiety, the *stability* of the personality is both its most cherished asset and its most powerful handicap. I wrote that the mind from this vantage point is an environment – a stable, relatively secure

world in which the schizoid individual lives. He is oriented toward keeping it from being rearranged by the outside, but also towards making it as personally interesting and cozy to live in as possible. Insularity, self-containment, and an avoidance of spontaneity or surprise are therefore quite important. A boundary is built between the inner world and the outer world to *prevent* a free and spontaneous interchange beyond the already known and the relatively predictable and controllable. . . . I had no idea at the time that I was writing about what I would later come to see as a dissociative defense against the "shock" of trauma and potential retraumatization.

(Bromberg, 1998:8–9)

Bromberg sees the withdrawal of the self from external reality as *the major source of self-protection from the possibility of future traumatization*. Fairbairn was focused on the trauma to the child if it was able to recognize that his/her parents were unloving and indifferent to his/her well being, thus provoking an abandonment crisis, while Bromberg has expanded the types of trauma to include the possibility of the child experiencing overwhelming "annihilation anxiety", which has the potential to obliterate the child's functioning personality.

Another source that drives the child away from external relationships is that the child whose needs are repeatedly rejected assumes that he has been asking for too much because his legitimate needs have been ignored time after time. His unmet emotional needs continue to demand satisfaction and each time he asks for support and love and is rejected he loses another modicum of his dignity. The child or youth faced with parents like the ones Fairbairn described turns into himself to protect his self-esteem from being further abused, and focuses on his inner world for all of his satisfactions, which are only partially satisfactory. Note that the same child is (paradoxically) increasingly dependent on his parental objects as they have not offered him enough support to promote differentiation.

Fairbairn then explicitly noted in his 1941 paper that children who are faced with a harsh and unsupportive external reality turn inward and seek "substitutive" satisfactions. This is the prime feature of the individual's "inner world", to which the child turns as a shelter from the harsh and ungiving reality in which he lives:

Frustration of his desire to be loved as a person and to have his love accepted is the greatest trauma that a child can experience, and it is this trauma above all that creates fixations in the various forms of infantile sexuality to which a child is driven in a resort as an attempt to compensate by substitutive satisfactions for the failure of his emotional relationships with his outer objects. Fundamentally, these substitutive satisfactions (e.g. masturbation and anal eroticism) all represent *relationships with internalized objects, to which the individual is compelled to turn in default of satisfactory relationships with objects in the outer world.*

(Fairbairn, 1941:39–40 italics in the original)

Fairbairn's amazingly accurate formulation preceded the advent of video games by at least 40 years, which today fascinates thousands upon thousands of young people who are isolated from others in their homes, and who become completely engulfed in a fantasy world that offers them some partial satisfaction for their unmet needs. Today, the unloved child or teen can attempt to nurture their underdeveloped sense of self with internal fantasies enhanced by an endless number of video games, where their frustrated needs for self-worth and significance, for a sense of personal power and for a feeling of control over their life can be partially satisfied. These partial satisfactions can be obtained by the undifferentiated child or adolescent without exposing themselves to the harsh emotional realities of the family in which they live, or worse, to objects in external reality. This turn inwards, with the replacement of reality with fantasy, can be seen as the starting point of many varieties of psychopathology, as fantasy is substituted for relational attachments to external objects. Anders Breivik, the Norwegian mass murderer who killed 77 of his fellow citizens, spent a total of five years playing the video game "World of Warcraft" as the leader of a guild (team) of players who played continuously for 12 to 16 hours a day. During this time he lived with his mother, who had abused him continually in his childhood. His complete focus on his fantasy world led to abandonment of all his friends, and eventually to the loss of his ability to self-care (Celani, 2020)

The satisfactions that substitute satisfactions do provide the isolated child are partial at the very best, as Fairbairn explains in the following clear and persuasive passage from his 1946 paper:

On the other hand, from the point of view of object-relationship psychology, explicit pleasure-seeking represents a deterioration of behavior. . . . Explicit pleasure seeking has as its essential aim the relieving of the tension of libidinal need for the mere sake of relieving this tension. Such a process does, of course, occur commonly enough: but since libidinal need is object need, simple tension-relieving implies some failure of object-relationships. The fact is that simple tension relieving is really a safety valve process. It is thus, not a means of achieving libidinal aims, but a means of mitigating the failure of these aims.

(Fairbairn, 1946:139–140)

Fairbairn's descriptions and explanations are "genteel" in that they do not emphasize the violence or extreme trauma that some children experience during their childhoods which drives them to seek shelter in their inner world of fantasy gratification. The following quote by Rehberger (2014) graphically describes the ordeals to which children are exposed, and demonstrates that Fairbairn's basic premises and positions are still in the literature today, although, typically, without any mention of his contributions.

Infants and toddlers are overwhelmed when faced with inadequate care, neglect of their basic needs, or violence. If their cry for help is not heard, this deprivation leads them to suffer feelings of helplessness and even fear of impending death. When they cry in need of care, comfort, safety, and help, when they are hungry or in pain and are subsequently yelled at shaken, beaten, hurt, strangled, bound, or put aside without being provided for, their despair increases exponentially. If they are forced to eat, sleep, defecate, or are painfully restricted in their quest for knowledge they will permanently feel overwhelmed and threatened by demands, reprimands, and instructions. Repeatedly sustained helplessness in combination with the fear of death is permanently stored within their emotional memory. It can be reactivated within the adult by an existential crisis and drastically worsen the subjective perception of the present-for example anxiety – and panic attacks induced by remote or non-existent danger. . . . Fears are suppressed and the child no longer anticipates any help. He no longer seeks intimacy in relationships. He suppresses his desire to bond, suppresses his fear and grief, even his anger, and then shuts down. This results in the typical schizoid retreat to the inner world of internalized object relations.

(Rehberger, 2014:462)

This quote breathes life into Fairbairn's dry and clinical descriptions of children's experiences of trauma. It illustrates how completely devastating it can be to the child's developing personality. Rehberger follows up on the first quote by highlighting the consequences to the child's future emotionality in the following passage:

> Many try to escape the grief by identifying with the bully and bash-fully laughing – all the while experiencing emotional pain. They should be crying. Without the knowledge of grief and tears, rela-tionships become empty, comfort is not to be found in empathic people, compassion with oneself and also with others is absent. . . . The hopes for empathy, respect and comfort from others are no longer nourished. They remain desolate, desperate and hopeless. The unconsoled and wary can only turn to themselves for help, since they mistrust others. They no longer rely on others to attain security; they shut down, pull away and only accept superficial encounters.
>
> (Rehberger, 2014:463)

This powerful description of the schizoid represents a huge cohort of patients, most of whom live lives of social isolation and behave hyper-autonomously, gratifying their every whim, and never allowing external relationships to interfere with their attempts to continuously meet their needs. Fairbairn noted in his discussion of defenses that one of the three fundamental defenses was the attempt by the individual to keep external objects from "breaching" the wall around his inner world, and assigned that very difficult task to the analyst (Fairbairn, 1958:374–385).

Fairbairn on Differentiation

Fairbairn discussed the process of differentiation in his second theo-retical paper, *A Revised Psychopathology of the Psychoses and Psy-choneuroses*, published in 1941. Fairbairn had previously noted that the rejected, ignored or under-nurtured child was more, rather than less, attached to his object, thus leading to developmental arrest. He begins his discussion of the normal process of differentiation within his metapsychology in the following quote:

> It is one of the chief conclusions to which I have been led by the study of cases displaying schizoid features that the development

of object-relationships is essentially *a process whereby infantile dependence upon the object gradually gives place to mature dependence upon that object*. This process of development is characterized (a) by the gradual abandonment of an original object-relationship based upon primary identification, and (b) by the gradual adoption of an object-relationship based on differentiation of the object.

(Fairbairn, 1941:34)

Despite many digressions within his 1941 paper, he observed that patients who have been deprived or neglected and who have developed a schizoid style are fearful of entering the world of external objects.

The great conflict of the transition stage may be formulated as a conflict between a progressive urge to surrender the infantile attitude of identification with the object with a regressive urge to maintain that attitude. During this period, accordingly, the behavior of the individual is characterized both by desperate endeavors on his part to separate himself from the object and desperate endeavors to achieve reunion with the object-desperate attempts "to escape from prison" and desperate attempts "to return home".

(Fairbairn, 1941:43)

This description can be observed in many overly dependent young adult patients whose first venture outside the family is an often-futile attempt to sell products to relatives and friends because presenting himself/herself to an employer is beyond his/her ability. When success eludes the young adult, they often resume his/her dependency position and may give up on attempts to emerge into the world of external objects. In Fairbairn's metapsychology, the source of the schizoid's excessive dependency is very clear. It is an early interpersonal environment in which the child did not receive enough love, support and encouragement to separate from his objects in a stepwise manner which results in an inability to explore the world of external objects.

The following shortened quote reflects Suttie's previously noted position that the child has to be sure of continuing support from his parents even if he/she does not need to call upon them.

The greatest need of a child is to obtain conclusive assurance (a) that he is genuinely loved as a person, and (b) that his parents genuinely accept this love. It is only insofar as such assurance is forthcoming in a form sufficiently convincing to enable him to depend safely upon his real objects that he is able to gradually renounce infantile dependence without misgiving. In the absence of such assurance his relationship to his objects is fraught with too much *anxiety over separation* to enable him to renounce the attitude of infantile dependence; for such a renunciation would be equivalent in his eyes to forfeiting all hope of ever obtaining the satisfaction of his unsatisfied emotional needs.

(Fairbairn, 1941:39)

Clinically, there are numerous examples of under-nurtured schizoid adults of both genders who live at home and who only venture out into the world in small ways, but remain attached to their ungiving objects. Others who have moved out remain attached by calling home every day, having breakfast daily at home or accepting money from their parents while not achieving their potential in their work. Fairbairn's analysis of this type of patient remains relevant today.

A New Vision of the Human Unconscious

Fairbairn addressed a large number of separate but overlapping issues in his 1943 paper, *Repression and the Return of Bad Objects (with special reference to the "War Neuroses")*. First, he revised the purpose, the operations and finally contents of the human unconscious, a reformulation which is completely unrelated to Freud's description of the unconscious. He also described his first non-dissociative defense, called "The Moral Defense Against Bad Objects", as well as one of the three major structural defenses used to avoid encountering previously dissociated and then repressed toxic memories. He also offered a clear and logical definition of the continuum of severity of psychopathology, along with noting the power inherent in the "good object" in the treatment situation. It is the most dense and multifaceted chapter that he ever produced, as his ideas were emerging at an enormous rate.

Fairbairn begins the chapter with the startling assertion that libido was "object seeking", and that the relationship between the child and his object was more important than libidinal gratification.

Amongst the conclusions formulated in the above-mentioned paper (1941) two of the most far reaching are the following: (1) that libidinal "aims" are of secondary importance in comparison with object-relationships, and (2) that a relationship with the object, and not gratification of impulse is the ultimate aim of libidinal striving. These conclusions involve a complete recasting of the classic libido theory: and in the paper in question an attempt is made to perform this task.

(Fairbairn, 1943:60)

This is one of the revolutionary statements that Fairbairn made throughout his work. His assertion requires him to present a different version of psychoanalysis to the reader, one that covers the same areas as classical psychoanalysis: psychopathology, personality development, differentiation, integration, the operation of the unconscious, resistance, transference, defenses as well as a model of treatment. It is a very long and complex list of topics, and he began the task by addressing his view of the development and dynamics of the human unconscious. He rejected Freud's belief that repression was based on Oedipal guilt and replaced it with the child's fear of and revulsion toward the toxicity of the bad object in relation to his/her developing ego.

I now venture to formulate the view that *what are primarily repressed are neither intolerably guilty impulses nor intolerably unpleasant memories, but intolerably bad internalized objects*. If memories are repressed accordingly, this is only because the objects involved in such memories are identified with bad internalized objects; and, if impulses are repressed, this is only because the objects with which such impulses impel the individual to have a relationship are bad objects from the standpoint of the ego.

(Fairbairn, 1943:62)

This is Fairbairn's re-definition of the human unconscious in terms of object relations theory. Sexuality, drive, inherited aggression and Oedipal guilt have nothing to do with Fairbairn's vision of the human unconscious. Fairbairn's unconscious is created by the dissociation of memories that had the potential to trigger fear of abandonment. He saw the human unconscious as being accrued over time, and that it varies in strength from individual to individual based on the number and intensity of traumatic experiences to which any given child had been exposed. He then turned to the example of children who were sexually assaulted, and described his view of the relationship between trauma and dissociation:

> At one time I used to frequently have the experience of examining problem children; and I remember being particularly impressed by the reluctance of children who had been the victims of sexual assaults to give any account of the traumatic experiences to which they had been subjected. The point which puzzled me the most was that, the more innocent the victim was, the greater was the resistance to anamnesis. . . . At that time, I felt that these phenomena could only be explained on the assumption that, in resisting the revival of the traumatic memory, the victim of a sexual assault was actuated by guilt over the unexpected gratification of libidinal impulses which had been renounced by the ego and repressed. . . . I had always felt rather suspicious of this explanation; but it seemed the best available at the time.
>
> (Fairbairn, 1943:63)

In this quote, Fairbairn is working his way toward a trauma/dissociation model, which became the basis of his view of the genesis of the unconscious. In the case of a sexual assault, the child's motivation for not remembering is not based on guilt from (assumed) gratification, but from horror and a desire to not experience retraumatization.

The trauma need not be as great as a sexual assault, but rather "cumlative trauma", repeated small rejections by the parents of the child's legitimate needs that can damage the child's ego over time. Fairbairn finishes off the prior quote with his conclusion relating to the internalization of bad objects:

> As I now see it, the position is that the victim of a sexual assault resists the revival of the traumatic memory primarily because this memory represents a record of a relationship with a bad object. . . . It is intolerable in the main, not because it gratifies repressed impulses, but for the same reason that a child flies panic-striken from a stranger who enters the house. It is intolerable because a bad object is always intolerable, and a relationship with a bad object can never be contemplated with equanimity.
>
> (Fairbairn, 1943:63)

Fairbairn then concluded that psychopathology was the result of the number, intensity and frequency of intolerably frustrating and need-rejecting events that the child had experienced in childhood. Rejections are present to some degree in all childhood histories; however, the key difference is that each child experiences a different frequency and intensity of parental empathic failures.

> At one time it fell to my lot to examine quite a large number of delinquent children from homes which the most casual observer could hardly fail to recognize as "bad" in the crudest sense – homes for example, in which drunkenness, quarrelling and physical violence reigned supreme. It is only in the rarest instances, however, (and those only instances of utter demoralization and collapse of the ego) that I can recall such a child being induced to admit, far less volunteering, that his parents were bad objects. It is obvious that in these cases the child's bad objects had been internalized and repressed. . . . For that matter, it also applies to the ostensibly "normal" person. It is impossible for anyone to pass through childhood without having bad objects which are internalized and repressed. Hence internalized bad objects are present in the minds of all of us at deeper levels.
>
> (Fairbairn, 1943:64–65)

No child has a perfect or carefree childhood, so in every history there are events in which the child became inconsolable. In supportive, loving households these negative events still have to be dissociated, but because of their lack of frequency, as well as the presence of a much larger number of good object memories, they are unable to exert much influence on the inner world.

The Influence of Internalized Bad Objects: Fairbairn's Definition of the Origins of Psychopathology

Fairbairn then explained why some individuals develop and display psychopathology while others do not. Fairbairn's definition emerges straightforwardly from the earlier definitions of dissociated interpersonal trauma and is logical and consistent with his model of the human psyche as one that is built by internalizing external relationships, good and bad alike:

> Whether any given individual becomes delinquent, psychoneurotic, psychotic or simply "normal" would appear to depend in the main

upon the operation of three factors: (1) The extent to which bad objects have been installed in the unconscious and the degree of badness by which they are characterized, (2) The extent to which the ego is identified with internalized bad objects, and (3) The nature and strength of the defenses which protect the ego from these objects.

(1943:64)

This interpersonal definition is elegant and clear. The child exposed to high levels of trauma, be it rejection of their needs, physical abuse or continuous indifference, will experience more psychopathology in adulthood than comparable children who experienced low levels of trauma and whose unconscious is not populated by hundreds if not thousands of dissociated and then repressed memories of traumatic events. Those children identified with the abuser(s) will be more prone to act out and find new victims for their dissociated rage, and children who were disidentified with their object will be vulnerable to recurring struggles with their internalized memories of past intolerable experiences, as the following example from my practice illustrates.

I worked with a patient who had a chronically traumatic childhood which included poverty and a brutal father. They lived in a mobile home community, and when she was eight or nine years old a feral dog gave birth to a litter of puppies at the edge of their property. Her father grabbed his gun and began shooting the puppies, to the absolute horror of his daughter. His son was excited about the event and asked his father if he could shoot one, and he was encouraged to do so. When all the puppies had been killed my patient ran outside in a futile effort to save them but ended up burying them. This severe example illustrates Fairbairn's first and second points regarding the development of psychopathology. Both children were exposed to the horrific scene, but the son who identified with his father participated in it, while my patient was repulsed and still traumatized by the event years later. It also highlights the horrors that many apparently "ordinary" patients have experienced during their developmental histories.

Fairbairn continued to discuss his views on the internalization of bad objects in his 1943 paper, specifically, bad objects from the child's own family as opposed to violent strangers. He recognized that the child, who was completely dependent on his objects, had no choice but to internalize them despite the fact that they were "bad", i.e., unsatisfying of the child's needs and thus frustrating. Note that Fairbairn was

still assuming that only bad objects were internalized, a position that
he (partially) gave up in in his 1951 *Addendum* paper:

> However much he may want to reject them, he cannot get away from
> them. They force themselves upon him; and he cannot resist them
> because they have power over him. He is accordingly compelled
> to internalize them in an effort to control them. But in attempting
> to control them in this way, he is internalizing objects which have
> wielded power over him in the external world; and these objects
> retain their prestige for power over him in the inner world. In a
> word, he is "possessed" by them as if by evil spirits.
>
> (Fairbairn, 1943:67)

Fairbairn, not surprisingly, uses religious imagery frequently, a legacy
of his early studies to become a minister. He assumed that the child
wants to control his bad objects because when he is alone, abandoned
or being criticized, he can turn to his inner world and find his internal
objects that are always present and are not as threatening as the parent may be in the external world. Thus his inner world serves to mitigate his feelings of abandonment. This minor comfort derived from
his internalized objects is better than engaging with the harsh external
reality and being re-traumatized yet again. Fairbairn then highlights
the fact that the child's absolute dependency on his objects forces him
to accept and internalize his bad objects, even if they are neglectful.

> The child not only internalizes his bad objects because they force
> themselves upon him and he seeks to control them, but also, and
> above all, because he *needs* them. If a child's parents are bad
> objects, he cannot reject them, even if they do not force themselves
> upon him; for he cannot do without them. Even if they neglect him,
> his need for them is increased.
>
> (Fairbairn, 1943:67)

The child's increased need for the rejecting parent comes from the fact
that he has not received enough love and support to differentiate, and has
no choice to wait until he is able to risk separating from them and entering the world of external objects. The key observation here is that deprivation leads to *increased attachment* to the bad object. In Fairbairn's
metapsychology a bad object is defined as a parent or caretaker from
whom the child seeks love and support and is continuously rejected by

that person who fails to meet the child's legitimate dependency needs. This is one of his fundamental ideas that has come down from Fairbairn into current models: that development and differentiation depend on continuous and early support from the parents that allows the child to risk leaving his mother's side and venture into the world around him. As time goes on in the life of a deprived child, the early unmet needs do not disappear, but rather they are added to the current needs that are not being met, and the child falls further and further behind his peers who have been raised in more nurturing families.

The Moral Defense Against Bad Objects

Fairbairn described a cognitive defense in his 1943 paper that the child uses to hide from the realization that he is being neglected, humiliated or abused within his family. This defense appears after the child develops a sense of logic and cause and effect. Fairbairn called this defense "The Moral Defense Against Bad Objects". This is another concept of Fairbairn's that came from Suttie (1935:34–35), in his discussion of keeping the mother's love at any cost. I am always ambivalent about this defense because it is based on Fairbairn's mistaken belief that good objects are only internalized to "buffer" bad internal objects (Fairbairn, 1943:66). He assumed that internalization was a defensive act, rather than a normal process of experiencing the world. The Moral Defense is actually a primitive example of splitting in which the child makes himself "all bad", which effectively removes all the onus from his parents for being abusive or neglectful. Another source of ambivalence for me about this defense is that Fairbairn's finest quote (often the only quote that is remembered by individuals in the analytic community) is found in the section describing the moral defense, which is not central to his model, and which he ignored after he developed his structural model of 1944. It is true that many patients identify themselves as the "bad seed" and believe that their parents are completely innocent and are thus mystified by their own "irrational" misbehavior, which gives the Moral Defense its face value and appeal.

Fairbairn begins his discussion with his observation that delinquent children try to keep their parents "good" by accepting the blame for all that has gone wrong in their life:

If the delinquent child is reluctant to admit that his parents are bad objects, he by no means displays equal reluctance to admit that he himself is bad. It becomes obvious therefore, that the child would rather be bad himself than have bad objects: and accordingly we have some justification for surmising that one of his motives in becoming "bad" is to make his objects "good". In becoming "bad" he is really taking upon himself the burden of badness which appears to reside in his objects. By this means he seeks to purge them of their badness, and, in proportion as he succeeds in doing so he, is rewarded by that sense of security which an environment of good objects so characteristically confers. . . . Outer security is purchased at the expense of inner insecurity; and his ego is now at the mercy of a band of fifth columnists or persecutors.

(Fairbairn, 1943:65)

Fairbairn then indulges in a speculative chain of hypotheses regarding the difference between "conditional" and "unconditional" badness. He assumed that the child forcibly internalized good objects to buffer his internalized bad objects, and thus make himself conditionally bad, as opposed to unconditionally bad. This was the only time that Fairbairn spoke of internalizing good objects (up to the revision of the *Addendum* of 1951), a belief that was influenced by the work of Klein. He saw the motivation for internalizing good objects as an attempt by the individual to modify his unconditional badness and becoming "Morally Bad," which was a less severe state of affairs (Fairbairn, 1943:66). His reasoning is "explained" by a series of hypothetical speculations, none of which has any footing in reality. In the following quote he compares unconditional badness to moral badness. This distinction is based on the ability of the child to correct moral badness, whereas unconditional badness is inescapable. Overall, this quote is clearly his best-remembered from all of his works.

Framed in such terms the answer is that it is better to be a sinner in a world ruled by God than to live in a world ruled by the Devil. A sinner in a world ruled by God may be bad; but there is always a sense of security derived from the fact that the world around is good. – "God's in His Heaven – All's right with the world!" and in any case there is always hope of redemption. In a world ruled by the Devil the individual may escape the badness of being a sinner, but he is bad because the world around him is bad. Further he can have no sense of security and no hope of redemption. The only prospect is one of death and destruction.

(Fairbairn, 1943:66–67)

As mentioned, there is face value to this defense; however, it is equally probable that a child's assumption that he is "bad" is the result of the internalization of hundreds and hundreds of hostile, abusive projections which were forced onto the child by his parents during his development. These projections accumulate in his unconscious structures and create his antilibidinal ego, which in turn influences his self presentation and his interactions with external objects. To support this alternative view of the development of the Moral Defense, Kopp (1978), an existential psychologist, demonstrates his internalization of hostile projections, as well as idealization of his punitive parents, in the following quotes.

> Bemuddled by years of immersion in an atmosphere of family hypocrisy, I had emerged from adolescence believing that I was an awful, inadequate human being who went around making other people unhappy. It was the only way I could account for being condemned by people as honest and good as my parents. I entered therapy to be cured of whatever failings had warranted their condemnation.
>
> (Kopp, 1978:86)

> Until I was twenty I had believed that my family had shamed and punished me because I was a bad child who had made everyone unhappy. With the help of my first therapist I gradually came to understand instead that the only reason I had been mistreated was because my mother hated me, and because my Father did not care to intervene.
>
> (Kopp, 1978:90)

The recognition by Kopp that his mother hated him is a rare insight that few patients can achieve. In my experience, patients who approach the reality that they were treated badly in childhood try to sidestep this conclusion by "understanding", rationalizing or making excuses for the abuse they received (Celani, 2005). As an example of patients who excuse their parents for their abuse, I will use a well-written literary example that protected the protagonist from an abandonment crisis, in Katherine Harrison's novel "Thicker Than Water".

> To myself I might say, "My mother was an unfulfilled person and unhappy". Or, "Mother always regretted that she didn't pursue her ballet". Or the more dangerous, "Mother loved me, she just wasn't

ready to have a child. It wasn't that she didn't love me, she was just young and selfish. It was because I reminded her of my father that she was sometimes unkind". I am rarely able to evaluate the truth of my words, or their importance. She loves me, she loves me not: the age old image of the suffering lover. After a certain excess of scrutiny, I was blinded by the looking.

(Harrison, 1991:88)

Fairbairn's model is supported both in the clinical setting and by authors who are completely unfamiliar with his work, but who describe the very same emotional reactions that Fairbairn first identified in his writing. I will use a number of writers and essayists throughout this work, all of whom speak directly about their emotional reactions, which seem to come directly from Fairbairn's model.

References

Bromberg, P. (1998). *Standing in the Spaces*. New York: Psychology Press.

Celani, D.P. (2005). *Leaving Home: How to Separate from Your Difficult Family*. New York: Columbia University Press.

Celani, D.P. (2020). Applying Fairbairn's object relations theory to the psychological development of Anders Breivik. *The Psychoanalytic Review*, 107 (4): 337–366.

Fairbairn, W.R.D. (1940). Schizoid factors in the personality. In *Psychoanalytic Studies of the Personality*. London: Routledge & Kegan Paul, 1952, pp. 3–27.

Fairbairn, W.R.D. (1941). A revised psychopathology of the psychoses and psychoneuroses. In *Psychoanalytic Studies of the Personality*. London: Routledge & Kegan Paul, 1952, pp. 28–58.

Fairbairn, W.R.D. (1943). The repression and return of bad objects (with special references to the "war neuroses"). In *Psychoanalytic Studies of the Personality*. London: Routledge & Kegan Paul, 1952, pp. 59–81.

Fairbairn, W.R.D. (1944). Endopsychic structure considered in terms of object relationships. In *Psychoanalytic Studies of the Personality*. London: Routledge & Kegan Paul, 1952, pp. 82–132.

Fairbairn, W.R.D. (1946). Object-relationships and dynamic structure. In *Psychoanalytic Studies of the Personality*. London: Routledge & Kegan Paul, 1952, pp. 137–151.

Fairbairn, W.R.D. (1951). Addendum. In *Psychoanalytic Studies of the Personality*. London: Routledge & Kegan Paul, pp. 133–136.

Fairbairn, W.R.D. (1958). On the nature and aims of psycho-analytical treatment. *International Journal of Psychoanalysis*, 39: 374.

Harrison, K. (1991). *Thicker Than Water*. New York: Random House.

Kopp, S. (1978). *An End to Innocence: Facing Life without Illusions*. New York: Bantam Books.

Rehberger, R. (2014). Viewing Camus's *The Stranger* from the perspective of W.R.D. Fairbairn's object relations. In Clarke, G. and Scharff, D. Eds., *Fairbairn and the Object Relations Tradition*. London: Karnac Books, pp. 461–470.

Suttie, I. (1935). *The Origin of Love and Hate*. London: Pelican Books.

Chapter 3

Trauma, Dissociation, Splitting and Fairbairn's Structural Theory

Early Trauma

Bromberg, who has written extensively on dissociation and trauma, sees the toxicity inherent in trauma as based on the fact that it disrupts the coherence and organization of the child's developing ego structure. In this first passage, he equates a traumatic event between parent and child as equivalent to a death of part of the child's personality. That is, the child's memory of himself during those toxic emotional interactions with his parent is dissociated along with the memory of the interaction, as well as his memory of the parent, as the event is too disruptive for the central ego to process and to accept.

> It is a defense against trauma, which unlike defenses against internal conflict, does not simply deny the self access to potentially threatening feelings, thoughts and memories: it effectively obliterates, at least temporarily, the *existence* of that self to whom the trauma could occur, and it is in a sense a "quasi-death". The rebuilding of linkages, the reentry into life, involves pain not unlike that of mourning. The return to life means the recognition and facing of death: not simply the death of one's early objects as real people, but the death of those aspects of self with which those objects have been united.
>
> (Bromberg, 1998:173)

This dramatic passage describes the destructive impact of a trauma-laden early childhood. Bromberg, unlike Fairbairn, does not focus on the child's motivation to dissociate intolerable memories of abuse and neglect in order to avoid feelings of abandonment, but

DOI: 10.4324/9781003394181-4

instead he focuses on the danger to the central ego of being over-whelmed by intense emotionality that threatens to destabilize and overrun the child's nascent ego structure. Bromberg's focus on the flood of emotion accompanying the terror of disintegration is a related and valuable addition to Fairbairn's original ideas regarding the neces-sity for dissociation. In both Fairbairn's and Bromberg's view, disso-ciation is triggered by massive anxiety that the child's central ego is not capable of facing without enduring overwhelming consequences.

> Psychological trauma occurs in situations, explicitly or implicitly interpersonal, in which self invalidation (sometimes self *annihila-tion*) cannot be escaped from or prevented and from which there is no hope of protection, relief or soothing. If the experience is either prolonged assaultively violent, or if self-development is weak or immature, then the level of affective arousal is too great for the event to be experienced self-reflectively, and given mean-ing through cognitive processing. . . . At its extreme, the subjec-tive experience is that of a chaotic and terrifying flooding of affect that threatens to overwhelm sanity and psychological survival, but to one degree or another its shadow is an inherent aspect of what shapes mental functioning in every human being.
>
> (Bromberg, 1998:12)

Bromberg sees that the dissociative defense affords the child protection from the possibility that his nascent central ego will be overwhelmed. In the following quote, he notes how the defense of dissociation pre-vents this from occurring.

> The essential nature of trauma is that because the person is not pre-pared to cope with it, the integrity of the ego is passively over-whelmed, and the experience of "being oneself" begins to fragment and depersonalize. It is in this sense that dissociation protects against self-fragmentation and restores personhood and sanity by hypnoidally unlinking the incompatible states of consciousness and allowing access to them only as discontinuous and cognitively unrelated mental experiences.
>
> (Bromberg, 1998:260)

One of the three aforementioned early patients of mine who displayed independent dissociated self-states was the daughter of a violent, emotionally primitive and aggressive man who, when angered, pulled the telephone off the wall or tipped the refrigerator over and stomped on the food that had fallen to the floor. She also described to me how she would be disciplined when her father was enraged at her. He would put her in the car and drive slowly around the neighborhood roaring at her with all of his fury. She would begin to cry, which would seem to excite him, and he would redouble his efforts. At some point, she would feel herself dissolve into pure terror which would appease her sadistic father and he would then drive home. Her description of "dissolving" was equivalent to the collapse of her selfhood described by Bromberg. Not surprisingly, in our sessions she demonstrated almost complete dissociation of any emotions attached to those incidents of trauma and bland indifference regarding the intensity of "badness" of her objects. Surprisingly (to me), she would drive back to her home of origin on most weekends to help her now-elderly parents do weekly chores, completely unaware of the traumas that she experienced there. In between our weekly sessions I would often receive a long handwritten letter saying that I was right about the level of her father's violence toward her and about the chaos of her childhood. I was new to the field, but I recognized that I was dealing with two unintegrated and completely separate self-states. This severe splitting continued for many, many months and I became frustrated by the two separate, nearly opposite realities that my patient was presenting. During one session, when my patient was in her libidinal ego state (seeing her father and mother in an unrealistic positive light), I produced one of her letters with the intention of reading parts of it back to her. She became instantly enraged and said that she was going to get out of her chair and slap me in the face, whereupon I tucked the letter away. I learned that there is simply no tampering with the rigid and split-off sub-egos until the analyst or therapist has been identified by the patient's central ego as an ally and as a source of emotional support.

There is another factor in the child's inability to see the parent as a single object which is parental chaos and instability. When discussing psychoanalytic models the language tends to be clinical and "cool", but children raised in chaos and violence experience traumatic incidents that are extreme and are whitewashed by clinical description. The following passage is by Blizard (2019), who describes the conditions experienced by children who later developed borderline personality disorders and who were more violently and intensely rejected than those that Fairbairn described in his writings. Here, Blizard notes that the chaotic ever changing parent is impossible to internalize as a single person, so the child contains many realistic, yet mutually dissociated and contradictory visions of their parent.

> Attachment relationships with caregivers who are dissociative, psychotic or sociopathic involve thousands upon thousands of frightening, double-binding interactions that may impair the development of reality testing in a more pervasive and insidious manner than discreet traumatic events. Such contradictory relationships lead to disorganized attachment in infants, a condition that predicts dissociation from childhood into young adulthood. . . . The child may need to form dissociated, i.e. split, mental representations of good and bad aspects of the self in relationship to the caregiver. . . . These contradictory attachment patterns cannot be integrated into whole self and object representations, impairing the interpretation of people's appearance, intentions, and behavior. . . . A parent's distorted or fragmented model of reality may actively discourage the use of important modes of reality testing needed to construct an integrated view of the world. Children need repeated interactions with adults who can articulate and empathize with the child's experiences as well as differentiate them from their own. . . . When the parental relationship is pervasively abusive and lacking in empathy for the child's perceptions, the child may develop a narcissistically closed system of self nurturance.
>
> (Blizard, 2019:368–369)

In this quote, written 75 years after Fairbairn's structural paper of 1944, Blizard supports Fairbairn's observations regarding the consequences to the child's ego structure of failed parenting in terms of relational skills and the difficulty of integration of dissimilar part objects. It demonstrates how many of Fairbairn's once-radical ideas and major themes are revived in this quote, including the dissociation of repeated toxic memories of traumatic parental failures, the resulting splitting of the object into separate objects that that relate to part selves of the child, and the parent's unregulated reality testing, which offers no consistent model for the development of the child's own reality testing.

The consequence of either a hostile, chaotic or psychotic parent leaves the child in an extremely vulnerable position in regard to his/her ego structure. In order to preserve a core aspect of the self, dissociation is used to isolate memories that would potentially disrupt the self.

In the following passage, Bromberg cites how self-preservation of the central ego results from splitting off incompatible experiences into independent sub-selves, a concept closely allied with Fairbairn's concept that isolated self states served to prevent integration, thus protecting the central ego from seeing both the good and bad parts of the object at the same time. Were this to occur, the enormity of the memories of parental "badness" would easily overwhelm the fewer events of emotional support and empathy that the child had experienced. The dissociated toxic memories would shatter the attachment of the patient to his/her object long before he/she could face the world independently.

> In other words, dissociation as a defense, even in relatively normal personality structure, limits self reflection to what is secure or needed for survival of selfhood, while in individuals for whom trauma has been severe, self-reflection is extremely curtailed in order that the capacity to reflect does not break down completely and result in a collapse of selfhood. . . . Thus paradoxically, the defensive division of the self into unlinked parts preserves identity by establishing more secure boundaries between self and "not-self" through dissociative unlinking of self states, each with its own boundaries and its own firm experience of not-self.
>
> (Bromberg, 1998:12)

It appears very unlikely that events that terrify the child to the point that they have to be dissociated can occur in "normal" personality structures. The following is an example from my own experience. I was speaking to a social acquaintance who knew that I was a psychologist, and he told me that he had a disturbing event with his five-year-old son. He told me that he was intensely angry at his son and was yelling loudly when his son looked up in terror and said, "Daddy, are you going to kill me?" That statement shocked my friend, who immediately stopped his aggression towards his son, realizing how terrified his little boy was. His child's assumption that he was going to be killed was far beyond what his father had intended, but events such as these (even when they occur in a normally supportive family) require the child to dissociate the memory of the event and hold it in his unconscious.

Both Fairbairn and Bromberg assume that the split off sub-selves allow the survival and *continuation* of a central sense of self, as the sub-selves "hide" critically disruptive information from dissolving the central ego. The consequence of a multiplicity of egos is that each sense of self has its own view of reality, specifically its opinion of the parental objects and its interpersonal goal toward that specific object. This position is described by Bromberg in the following passage.

> Because the individual states are defensively and rigidly isolated from one another, the dissociative structure has not only been restored but is now able to protect indefinitely the subjective sense of self consistency and continuity by locating personal identity tightly within whichever self-state has access to consciousness and cognition at any given moment.
>
> (Bromberg, 1998:12)

Bromberg notes that there are multiple sub-egos which effectively protect the central ego's sense of identity from disruption, as well as keeping the dissociated memories alive in these structures, which are key to treatment. One paradoxical "advantage" of dissociation followed by repression once the event is lodged in the unconscious is that the individual does not actually lose memories of what happened to him during childhood, but rather, these realities are preserved in his unconscious and remain alive in his psyche, along with the (painful) memory of his part-self that experienced the rejection. The "advantage" (if you could call it that) inherent in the preservation of painful memories is that at a later date, and with an attuned analyst, the memories of the dissociated parts of the self can be located, validated and become an accepted part of the central ego. Unfortunately, the destructive side of the splitting defense far outweighs its "advantage" in that the person appears to others to be inconsistent in the extreme, which produces a chaotic lifestyle, makes them a difficult employee and a mercurial friend, which often makes long-term relationships nearly impossible.

Steps in the Development of Fairbairn's Structural Model

Fairbairn described the earlier work of Janet in his 1954 paper, *Observation of the Nature of Hysterical States*, and used it in his explanation of his structural theory. This paper was published ten years after he had presented his structural theory in his 1944 paper *Endopsychic Structure Considered in Terms of Object Relationships*. He took hysteria as the prototype of the trauma/dissociation process and expanded it to encompass his approach to psychopathology and to the genesis of his structural theory.

> Janet's achievement was not confined, however, to a classification and description of hysterical symptomatology. It included an attempt to provide a scientific explanation of the genesis of the phenomena displayed by the hysteric; and the explanatory concept which Janet formulated was, of course, the classic concept of "dissociation". In terms of this concept the hysterical state is essentially due to an inability on the part of the ego to hold all the functions of the personality together, with the result that certain of these functions become dissociated from, and lost to, the rest of the personality and, having passed out of control of the ego, operate independently . . . the occurrence of such dissociations was attributed to the presence of certain weaknesses of the ego-weakness partly inherent, and partly induced by circumstances such as illness, trauma or situations imposing strain on the individuals capacity for adaptation.
>
> (Fairbairn, 1954:105–106)

This discussion of Janet demonstrates Fairbairn's thought process and the central role that dissociation plays in his model. For these separate and independent structures to exist, there must be a mechanism or process by which toxic parts of the original central ego have been "split" off the main structure forced into the unconscious, where they continue to exist independently of the central ego within the inner world. Fairbairn mistakenly assumed that dissociation was an aggressive act initiated by the central ego against the disruptive memory. The current assumption is that dissociation comes from massive anxiety, which is triggered by the content of the material in the specific memory that if understood consciously would overwhelm the capacity of the central ego to process it. In reality, the central ego is often depleted and is unable to control the split-off structures which are saturated with potent, emotionally overwhelming memories that can take over the executive function of the personality and repress the central ego.

Fairbairn's most direct statement about the "multiplicity of selves" appears in his 1944 paper as he was about to discuss his remarkable six-part structural theory.

> There (in the 1943 paper) I advance the view that repression is primarily exercised, not against impulses which have come to appear

painful or "bad" (as in Freud's final view) or even against painful memories (as in Freud's earlier view), but against *internalized
objects* which have come to be treated as bad. . . . How it may be
asked, can the ego be conceived repressing the ego? The answer
to this question is that, whilst it is inconceivable that the ego as a
whole should repress itself, it is not inconceivable that one part of
the ego with a dynamic charge should repress another part of the
ego with a dynamic charge.

(Fairbairn, 1944:90)

Here we can see the fundamental source of the structural theory – that
independent pairs of trauma-laden experiences, each with a self component and an object component and a powerful emotion linking them
are split off from the central ego. Both the dissociated part self and
the dissociated part object are too threatening to the existence of the
central ego to be accepted consciously, and remain independent from
the central core of the ego. The splitting defense allows the central ego
to exist without fear of disintegration. Were splitting to fail and the
individual's central ego be exposed to the overwhelming reality of his/
her childhood neglect or abuse, he/she would be ejected into a void
where he/she would not know what part of his childhood was real and
what was not, who he/she really is and worse, he/she would be cut off
from the only family that he/she knew, as Mitchell (1988) describes in
the following quote.

To abandon these bonds and entanglements is experienced as the
equivalent of casting oneself off from intense human contact altogether, an impossible option. Thus patients in analysis who are
beginning to sense the possibility of living and experiencing themselves and their worlds in a different way, are generally terrified of
profound isolation. To be different, even if that means to be open
to joyfulness and real intimacy with others, means losing ties to
internal objects which have provided an enduring sense of belong-
ing and connectedness, although mediated through actual pain and
desolation.

(Mitchell, 1988:28)

Mitchell is describing a powerful source of resistance – if the patient
gives up his bad objects, he fears that he will face a sense of aloneness
and isolation, regardless of the improvements that he will experience

in life. Until there is a viable alternative, that is, a new sense of self organized around the patient's relationship with the analyst, the bad objects will appear to be the better alternative, and the patient will remain attached to them.

The Two Pairs of Sub-Egos and Part Objects

Fairbairn described the steps in his thought processes that led him to the conclusion that there were multiple selves and objects in the individual's inner world in the following passage:

> Since it proves intolerable for him to have a good object which is also bad, he seeks to alleviate the situation by splitting the figure of his mother into two objects. Then, in so far as she satisfies him libidinally, she is a "good" object, and in so far as she fails him libidinally, she is a "bad" object. . . . He accordingly follows the only path open to him and, since reality is unyielding, he does his best to transfer the traumatic factor in the situation to the field of inner reality, within which he feels situations are more under his own control.
>
> (Fairbairn, 1944:110)

In this passage, Fairbairn continues to see internalization as a defensive process. Then, he recognized that the bad object was powerful because it displayed both rejection and allurement at different times. The emotionally abandoned child tries to sustain its love for the object by fantasizing that the parent contains a hidden storehouse of love that the child has not been able to discover. The bad object poses an insoluble problem for the child: it both rejects the child's needs, and moments later, the very existence of the parent in front of the child re-stimulates his/her longing for love and support. These two absolutely incompatible aspects of the bad object have to be split again into manageable emotional packages, as Fairbairn explains in the following passage:

> Unlike the satisfying object, the unsatisfying object (the bad object) has, so to speak, two facets. On the one hand it frustrates: and on the other hand, it tempts and allures. Indeed its essential "badness" consists precisely in the fact that it combines allurement with frustration. . . . As we have seen, in his attempt to deal with the intolerable

external situation with which he was originally faced his technique was to split the maternal object into two objects, (a) the "good" and (b) the "bad", and then proceed to internalize the bad object: and then in his attempt to deal with the intolerable internal situation which subsequently arises he adopts a technique which is not altogether dissimilar. He splits the internal bad object into two objects- (a) the needed exciting object and (b) the frustrating or rejecting object; and then he represses both of these objects (employing aggression of course, as the dynamic of repression).

(Fairbairn, 1944:111–112)

The second split of the rejecting/exciting object into two separate objects is based on the reality that no child can exist in a world completely filled with hate, rejection or indifference; there simply must be some hope of love. The first split off sub-ego, called the antilibidinal ego, "captures" and isolates the memories of the frightened, neglected and disappointed child in relation to his rejecting, indifferent or absent parent. The antilibidinal sub ego relates only to the internalization of the hostile, dismissive or neglectful behaviors that emerge from the parent, and Fairbairn called this internal structure the "rejecting object". This pair of part-self and part-objects are dissociated and remain in the unconscious, thus protecting the central ego from knowing how many times he/she experienced painful rejections.

The second sub-ego, called the "libidinal ego", relates only to those infrequent moments when the mother (or father) has offered some emotional support to the child, no matter how fleeting it may have been, which are then exaggerated. These partially true but enhanced events provide hope for the child in the future. The child's longing and hope, stimulated by the faintest amount of support, keeps the child focused on the parent as a potential source of emotional nurturance at some time in the future, despite the reality that the parent may have offered very little love to their child. The part of the parent that appeared to have the potential for love (as seen through the eyes of the libidinal ego) was called the "exciting object" by Fairbairn, as it ignited the child's hopes that he/she would be loved. Even a parent who is behaving in an indifferent manner allows the child to long for love from her and fantasize that her mother actually contains hidden love. The toxic aspect of the libidinal ego in relation to the exciting aspect of the parent is that the hoped-for support never (or hardly ever) comes to pass; it acts as a constant temptation that is just out of reach and is therefore intolerably frustrating. When the frustration builds from the object's lack of responsiveness to intolerable levels, the anxiety provokes the return of the antilibidinal ego/rejecting object view of the same parent. This concept, of a rejecting object and an exciting object that are responded to by two separate and isolated part-egos, is Fairbairn's single greatest contribution – it is the template for the borderline personality which has been virtually an unsolvable dilemma for other models to explain – yet here it is the very core of his model.

For his part, Fairbairn is the only major analytic theorist who saw that love from the parent was essential to emotional development and that the child created a fantasy of a loving object to sustain itself if love and support are absent in the environment. Secondly, he understood that the combination of allure and rejection emanating from the same object (the bad object) posed an insoluble problem for the child, requiring that dissociation be used to keep the opposite aspects of the object from encountering each other. Finally, the two sub-egos that develop in relation to the two part objects are each unwilling to give up on their deeply felt motivations: the pursuit of revenge or vindication (the antilibidinal ego), or of finding love in the object (the libidinal ego). These motives are separate (and opposite) objectives that neither sub-ego wants to abandon.

Fairbairn created his six-part structural theory by analyzing a patient's dream that has three egos and three related objects. Scharff (2014) has commented on Fairbairn's creative insight that led him to understand the relationships between the part selves and part objects in the patient's dream:

> Fairbairn recognized, in a moment of creative genius, that the ego, the executive aspect of the infant self, splits itself as well in relation to these internal objects, in order to release a part of itself to accompany the object and the affects associated with it into the unconscious and maintain its repression there, thus creating internal object relationships consisting of an ego and object bonded by the specific affect that has been overwhelming. These get sorted into two main categories – the libidinal (exciting) and (antilibidinal) internal object relationships. The antilibidinal ego is connected to the rejecting object and its feelings of anger at abandonment and rejection, while the libidinal ego is connected to the exciting object and its feelings of longing and craving.

> (Scharff, 2014:366)

Fairbairn assigned aggression to the part-self structure (the antilibidinal ego), and libido to the second part-self (love-seeking structure the libidinal ego). The motivation of both these structures comes from the relationship between the part-self and part-object (not from the central ego), and it is the source of attachment of the self and object structures to each other. The aggression of the antilibidinal ego is focused on the child's desire to "prove" himself/herself to be a valuable person to the negative and hostile rejecting object. This motivation creates a contentious and demanding sub-ego that engages the rejecting object in endless internal debates. Conversely, the libidinal ego sees the possibility of love in the exciting part object, no matter how abusive or neglectful the parent has been to him/her. This motivation is equally resistant to being given up by this substructure.

The great irony of Fairbairn's efforts is that he ended up producing a model that is antithetical to all of Freud's positions and assumptions, yet he used Freud's libidinal energy metaphor in his original formulation. He was clearly caught between his vision of the human psyche and the classical analytical model in which he had been trained. Thus, his new model was created using an older set of metaphors, and remarkably, it offers a completely different view of human psychology. Currently, Fairbairn's original speculations regarding the division of libidinal energies and aggression among the structures, and the dynamics regarding the assumed attacks between one structure against the others in the inner world have been eliminated from modern applications of his structural theory. What has emerged over time is a clear vision of human psychological functioning that is an alternative to the earlier metaphors that were used in its conception. It's simply hard to comprehend just how Fairbairn, with all his mixed metaphors and ungrounded speculations, came up with a model that is fundamentally so different from classical psychoanalysis.

The Development of the Central Ego and the Sense of Self

Fairbairn's structural theory begins with the child's alert and intact "Central Ego", which is conscious and relates to objects in reality, albeit in a simple and primitive manner. The central ego could remain unsplit in theory, assuming the infant never faced any frustration whatsoever and was never out of sight of his/her receptive mother – both of which are impossible. Thus, Fairbairn noted that everyone has some splitting of the ego, but it is on a continuum from mild to severe, depending upon the amount and intensity of frustration during development. All six structures in Fairbairn's model "grow" in the same way, in that they accrue memories of either support and love, or conversely of rejection and indifference, through thousands of interactions with their parents. Fairbairn assumed that the conscious structures were different from the four unconscious structures, and he did not see them as growing and maturing as a result of a relationship with a good object, which is a logical flaw in his model. Interestingly, he did recognize that the analyst's support of the underdeveloped central ego was a central part of treatment in his 1958 paper on psychotherapy, where he cited the role of the good object as a help to restart the patient's central ego's process of growth and maturity.

Every experience that the child has, either positive or negative, builds memories of interpersonal events that the child retains in fragmentary portions in different internal structures. Over time, repeated events with similar emotional tone (and with the same objects) form inner images of the child's self in relationship to his primary objects. It is also the way that the child begins to know himself, as repeated patterns of relationships in which he is defined in the same way by his objects create his/her self. A nuanced description of this point can be found in the following quote by Davies:

> Those patterns that repeat themselves with regularity – inherent representations and later fantasied elaboration of the most essential formative relationships – come to form a sense of character, order and agency They are that which makes us knowable to ourselves and others, despite the kaleidoscopic mélange of multiple selves. They order our world and create out of chaos, templates of personal meaning. . . . Such representational schemata, developmentally structured, become the filters through which all new experience is viewed, the system through which it will be organized, and the preexisting structure into which it must ultimately be integrated.
>
> (Davies, 1996, 562)

This is a good description of the mechanisms behind the development of the human character or personality, from an object relations theorist. Thus the human personality emerges largely from the interactive matrix of our internalized object relationships that appear frequently in the external world, as they interact with the child's inherent qualities, including intelligence, sensitivity and tolerance for stress.

Since Fairbairn's time, the emergence of the self has been redefined by a number of different writers in Object Relations Theory as an over-all "umbrella" that contains and relates to many sub-selves, all which are equally valid and relatively independent of each other. Bromberg calls the individual's unified sense of himself/herself an adaptive illusion in the following quote.

> There is now abundant evidence that the psyche does not start as an integrated whole but is nonunitary in origin – a mental struc-ture that begins and continues as a multiplicity of self-states that maturationally attain a feeling of coherence which overrides the awareness of discontinuity. This leads to the experience of a cohe-sive sense of personal identity, and the necessary illusion of being "one-self".
>
> (Bromberg, 1998:244)

Thus, the modern conception of the development of the self assumes that the central ego begins to identify itself in repeated themes and pat-terns that recur, and it weaves together a single identity which is able to connect all the familiar sub-selves into a single self.

Mitchell (2000) also contributed to the modern conception of the development of the self. He saw Fairbairn's original assumptions that the infant was born with an original unified and functional self as miss-ing the relational context from which the self emerges.

> Fairbairn started off on the wrong foot with regard to this ques-tion, because he did not fully appreciate the implications of view-ing the individual mind in a relational context with other minds. To pose the question, What is the motive for the first internali-zation? is to begin with the premise that there is a fundamental differentiation and boundary between inside and outside. This is a premise that Fairbairn inherited from Klein. If something from outside is found inside (which is what we mean by "internaliza-tion"), then we have to explain how it got there . . . What if a sense of oneself as a separate individual and objects as differenti-ated others is only gradually constructed, over the course of early development, out of this undifferentiated matrix? Then the sense

of oneself populated with presences of early significant objects would not have to be accounted for solely in terms of some discreet defensive process.

(Mitchell, 2000:109–111)

Mitchell's point here is that the sense of self is initially mixed with other objects and the realization that one is a separate individual develops gradually over time from a state of undifferentiation. Fairbairn's assumption that there exists a discrete and early functioning ego that singles out frustrating objects and then internalizes them as a defensive measure is no longer current and has been updated by this more sophisticated understanding.

The Central Ego and the Four Mostly Unconscious Structures

The fortunate child who is blessed with empathic and supportive parents will develop a central ego that is able to interact freely with objects in the external world, and his unconscious will contain relatively few (and weak) split-off parts that have been driven into his inner world as an escape from external reality. The child's central ego thrives on openness and nurturing memories which give it the courage to trust and to relate with objects in the external world, given its history of good experiences with its original objects. The richer the interpersonal matrix is with love and support, the stronger and more confident the central will become. From the Fairbairnian perspective, development comes down to the ratio of the number of positive, supportive and empathic interpersonal events the child encountered during development in contrast to the number of discouraging, indifferent or abandoning events with the parents that he encountered during his development. Note that it is possible for the unconscious structures to have more experience with parental rejection (far more in some cases) than the central ego has positive, supportive experiences with the good aspects of the same objects, resulting in the unconscious structures being *stronge*r and more saturated with motivation and purpose than is contained in the central ego. Thus, in individuals with toxic developmental histories, each of the four powerful unconscious part selves and part objects can take over the dominant executive position at any time, and each substructure will see the world through a self that is not shared with the rest of the personality.

The four mostly unconscious structures are grouped in two pairs, each having a self and object component that are tied together via intense emotionality, and relate to each other and only each other. They are simultaneously unaware of the other pair of split-off self and object, as well as of the central ego. The individual with a small number of positive interactions in its central ego will be unable to integrate the good and bad aspects of the object (as there are too many frightening and disruptive memories to metabolize), nor will it able to differentiate from his faulty objects as his developmental needs have not been met and he continues to focus on his still-needed object waiting for the needed support as his life slips away.

These two sets of mostly unconscious structures are filled with extreme emotions which can be seen firsthand when they are in the dominant ego structure and are able to express themselves interpersonally. This is why borderline patients are often avoided by clinicians. They simply do not want to face the extreme and uncompromising emotions that seem to take over the patient and create chaos in the consulting room. Skolnick (2014) has described the extremeness of these structures in the following quote, in which he characterizes the emotional intensity and single-mindedness of these structures as well as any writer in the analytic literature:

> Emotions, thoughts and even behaviors do not feel to be arising from a locus within the patient. Instead they are experienced as happening to the patient. As such, the truth of moment to moment psychic meaning, is for the patient, derived from an absolute eternal truth. The patient has no sense that they are in any way the arbiters of meaning, the master of their own perceptions. The contemptuous patient does not *imagine* you are a hopeless incompetent, they *know* that you are a hopeless incompetent, with no room for degrees of freedom. The adoring idealizing patient experiences the truth of his feelings similarly. Consequently his rancor towards or adoration of you is not debatable; it is the only reasonable response from a reasonable person whose reasoning follows from the absolute truth. Furthermore, since this organization contains split off islands of experience, in which time has collapsed into an eternal dimensionless plane, not only do the experiences of the paranoid/schizoid organization contain no past or future, there is no communication with the other states. The patient has no awareness that he possesses alternative feelings, or could imagine the

possibilities of other feeling perspectives at any point in time past or future.

(Skolnick, 2014:260)

This beautiful description offers an accurate feel of what dealing with a borderline entails. The absoluteness and extremeness of their perceptions makes debate about the reality of their opinions futile. As I have mentioned, I learned this firsthand with one of my first patients when I pulled out the letter she had written to me in a different ego state.

The Antilibidinal Ego/Rejecting Object Structure

No dependent child wants to consciously remember his/her state of terror, humiliation or abuse at the hands of his/her object. The child's antilibidinal ego's "strength" is dependent on the severity, duration and nature of the parent's rejection, be it physical abuse, sadism, indifference or contempt, thus creating a reservoir of resentment, rage and desire for revenge toward the parent in the unconscious structure. The rage, resentment and hostility of the antilibidinal ego cannot be underestimated. Beattie (2005) has noted how important revenge is as a motivation in abused individuals in the following passage:

> Revenge and vengeful fantasies may occur in many forms and on many levels, both conscious and unconscious, and may be expressed as readily through masochistic reaction formation as through overtly sadistic behavior. They have deep roots in early conflicts, traumas and humiliations at the hands of parents, siblings, and others. They need not however imply a primitive mode of object relatedness, for the vengeful person may demonstrate both a capacity for delay and self control, an empathic attunement to the victim's feeling and motivations.

(Beattie, 2005:513)

My experiences with patients who had powerful and massive antilibidinal ego structures were frequent and included a middle-aged man who was a successful stock broker and who came in with the presenting problem of his difficulties in his relationships with women. Our discussion soon moved on to his family history; he described himself as clumsy in the extreme, and as a child he had caused havoc in his family. He was one of three children, with an older brother and younger sister. His father was a failed businessman and alcoholic, who sadistically picked on my patient, telling him that he had a cruel streak, while his other two siblings were treated deferentially. In particular, his older brother was a talented athlete and his father allowed him privileges denied to my patient. As a child, my patient was so enraged about being unfairly punished that he used lighter fluid to ignite a carpet in his bedroom, which he quickly extinguished. His brother was a skilled oarsman who rowed their grandfather's rowing shell, and their father expressed pride in him. My patient was not allowed to touch it. He begged his father to teach him how to row, and his father finally agreed. One Saturday morning they went down to the dock for the lesson and his father was directing him on the technique for entering the light and narrow craft. As my patient was trying to follow instructions, he suddenly "slipped" and his foot punctured the light cedar planks of the boat, much to his father's despair and exasperation. His father then bought an English sports car, and he was forbidden to use it, but his older brother was allowed to drive it regularly. One weekend his father and brother was gone to the golf course earlier in the sports car, and my patient was to meet them later, using the family's old station wagon. While parking, my unconsciously enraged patient somehow managed to back the station wagon up and onto the hood of the new sports car in the large parking lot. After each accident, my patient was ashamed and contrite and apologized repeatedly, without any understanding of his motivation. Upon graduation from high school his father allowed him to take out the family sailboat with his friends for an evening sail on the lake. He was an experienced sailor and this was his graduation gift. He and his friends had an uneventful sail and when he returned home, his father asked him if he enjoyed himself and he replied in a most positive way. Within minutes the marina called and informed his father that the boat had sunk while tied to the dock. My patient had "forgotten" to re-fit the brass bailing plugs that allow water that gets into the cockpit to flow out as the boat is moving forward. A few years later, when the sports car was no longer a novelty, my patient was allowed to drive it, and did so with his foot on the floor. He was in a nearby city and came home at top speed, but noticed that the car was slower than normal and hesitating. Unbeknownst to his conscious ego, he had left the handbrake in the fully locked position, and the rear brakes were glowing hot. When he got back to town, the brakes were no longer being cooled by the high speed air flow and they melted the rubber seals which allowed the axle grease to flow onto the red hot brakes and the car burst into flames, consuming the rear fenders and trunk (Celani, 2005). This particular patient had an active and enraged antilibidinal ego structure of which he had absolutely no awareness, indicating extreme rejection from his father, and concurrently extreme dependency on him, as his father had not supported him enough to differentiate. His mother was described by this patient as another child in the family, who was unable to offer either safety or support. When a patient is attached to the rejecting object through revenge, he/she usually has an equally powerful libidinal ego that allows him/her to stay attached to such an aggressively rejecting object, which was the case. When his father became ill, he stayed with him and nursed him until he passed. Soon after he took his father's clothes and had them re-tailored to fit him to feel a closeness that he had never experienced in childhood. Over the years of my practice, I found that my patients offered me the most extreme examples of Fairbairn's structures that I could ever have imagined.

There is a continuous dialogue in the inner world of patients between the split-off self component and the object component. Not surprisingly, it is a continuation of the dialogue that was internalized from the external world and is now contained in the various structures. Ogden (2014), who has contributed significantly to the literature on Fairbairn, has described the dialogue between the rejecting object and the antilibidinal ego in the patient's inner world. Note that in Odgen's quote he continues to use the term "internal saboteur" to describe the child's traumatized self, a term that was changed to "antilibidinal ego" by Fairbairn in 1954.

> The relationship between the internal saboteur and the rejecting object derives from the infant's love of his mother despite (and because of) her rejection of him. . . . Neither the rejecting object nor the internal saboteur is willing to think about, much less relinquish, that tie. In fact, there is no desire on the part of either to change anything about their mutual dependence. The power of that bond is impossible to overestimate. The rejecting object and the internal saboteur are determined to nurse their feelings of having been deeply wronged, cheated, humiliated, betrayed, exploited, treated unfairly, discriminated against, and so on. The mistreatment at the hands of the other is felt to be unforgivable. An apology is forever expected by each, but never offered by either. Nothing is more important to

the internal saboteur than coercing the rejecting object into recognizing the incalculable pain that he or she has caused.

(Odgen, 2010:137–138)

The pathological attachment between the two members of each structure often serves as the most potent motivation in children and young
adults. The antilibidinal ego's single-minded goal is to either convince the rejecting object of his/her worth, or when this fails, to take
passive-aggressive revenge against them. When antilibidinal revenge
is added to the libidinal ego's opposite motivation to force love out of
the exciting object, Fairbairn's model shows us that these fundamental unconscious motivations create a remarkably powerful source of
attachment to the bad object, and of resistance to change.

The previous quote by Odgen describes a single individual's internal world. In the external world, the reality may have been quite different. For example, the "real" rejecting object parent may have been
absolutely indifferent and completely uninterested in the child from the
very beginning. However in the child's mind, *the parent must have had
a good reason for their rejection*, and we see this reflected in Odgen's
quote. The whole motivation of the antilibidinal ego is to prove itself
to be a valuable individual to the rejecting parent, or failing that, to
expose the parent to others as being "bad". The child's extreme emotions and single-minded motivation toward the rejecting object *demand
that the rejecting object parent has equal motivation*, which is not
necessarily the case. If the patient's central ego was able to recognize
that his/her parents couldn't care less about him/her, and in fact never
wanted a child in the first place, then this realization would render the
intense motivation of the antilibidinal ego as a complete illusion and a
waste of time. This recognition would collapse the entire inner world,
as the antilibidinal ego must "believe in" the validity of the rejecting
object's complaints just as the libidinal ego must believe that the exciting object does actually contain love. Thus the two self structures need
the two object structures to keep them motivated. The realization of
the patient that his objects were truly indifferent is seldom achieved
without help, as the antilibidinal ego's intense emotionality regarding
his need to prove himself or defeat the rejecting object as well as the
intense desire of the libidinal ego to find the love in the exciting object
keeps the whole personality structure stable and motivated.

So far, I have focused more on the antilibidinal ego than its "partner" structure, the rejecting object. However, the internal rejecting

object (an internalization of the rejecting parent) also has a view of the antilibidinal ego as an annoying, harassing, challenging and passive aggressive child. In the following passage, Ogden offers the view of the rejecting object toward the unwanted, disappointing child.

> From the point of view of the rejecting object (the split off aspect of self thoroughly identified with the mother), the experience of this form of pathological love involves the conviction that the internal saboteur (the antilibidinal ego) is greedy, insatiable, thin-skinned, ungrateful, unwilling to be reasonable, unable to let go a grudge, and so on. But despite the burdensomeness of the ceaseless complaining and self-righteous outrage of the internal saboteur, the rejecting object is both unwilling and unable to give up the relationship, that is to extricate itself from the mutual pathological dependence. The life, the determination, the very reason for being of the rejecting object (a part of the self) is derived from its tie to the internal saboteur.
>
> (Odgen, 2014:138)

This quote suggests that the rage and resentment of the antilibidinal ego keeps the rejecting object alive, and neither structure is willing to give up. In terms of the antilibidinal ego, its suspicion and hostility may be generalized to all those external objects who have power, and this pattern is projected into these new objects, thus recreating the same scenario in relationship after relationship.

Fairbairn's structures have been mentioned in literature and essays. One of the most interesting examples of a writer describing the dissociated rage in the antilibidinal ego comes from Katherine Anne Porter's essay "The Necessary Enemy" (1948), which I have cited in the past (Celani, 2010:90–91). In this short essay, Porter was able to recognize 70 years ago that underneath normal family relationships there could be dissociated rage that was unknown to the individual as a result of frustration in childhood. It is a remarkably astute essay from a woman who was not knowledgeable about psychoanalysis and was plagued with character issues throughout her life.

> She is a frank, charming, fresh hearted young woman who married for love. She and her husband are one of those gay, good looking young pairs who ornament the modern scene rather more in profusion than ever before in our history. They intend in all good faith

to spend their lives together, to have children and do well by them and each other – to be happy, in fact, which for them is the whole point of their marriage. . . . But after three years of marriage this very contemporary young woman finds herself facing the oldest and ugliest dilemma of marriage. She is dismayed, horrified, full of guilt and foreboding because she is finding out little by little that she is capable of hating her husband, who she loves faithfully. She can hate him at times as fiercely and mysteriously, indeed in terribly much the same way, as often she hated her parents, her brothers and sisters, whom she loved, when she was a child. Even then it had seemed to her a kind of black treacherousness in her, her private wickedness that, just the same, gave her her own private life. That was the one thing that her parents never knew about her, never seemed to suspect. For it was never given a name.

(Porter, 1948:182–183)

This quote is so filled with insight regarding dissociated antilibidinal rage that it speaks for itself. Porter must have discovered this structure in herself, through her own experience. One of the many insights in her essay is that rage toward objects that the individual feels he/she "should" love is unacceptable to the conscious self. She was also aware that hate toward the original parental objects was similar to hate toward current objects and was a result of various forms of frustration.

The Libidinal Ego/Exciting Object Structure

Fairbairn's work at the orphanage from 1927–1935 (Sutherland, 1989) exposed him to abandoned, desperate children, and he observed their deeply split views of their objects. He saw an ego state in these children that had no relation to reality, and as noted, he called it the "libidinal ego". Typically, Fairbairn changed the meanings of words that he borrowed from classical psychoanalysis. "Libidinal" in his metapsychology means seeking love and has nothing to do with sexuality and has no energetic substrate. When the child is dominated by this part-self state this sub-ego cannot see any "badness" in his/her objects, but rather is thrilled by all the promise of love that the parent seems to contain. This ego state, which is the other major player in the attachment to the bad object, is unique to Fairbairn's model and has not been improved upon since 1944. The libidinal ego was the ego state that I had seen repeatedly in my early work with my patients. It would suddenly appear when the patient was beginning to anticipate the possibility that they were emotionally abandoned and would shift from an antilibidinal-dominated view of their objects to the libidinal ego state that I originally called "Hope Springs Eternal". When dominated by this ego state, the child (or adult patient) is almost electrified by the hope that he/she can discover the pathway that will release the bountiful store of love and support that they fantasize is contained in one or the other of their parents. The libidinal ego-dominated patient is absolutely convinced that love awaits him/her, a belief which gives them continued hope, and which allows their attachment to continue uninterrupted. Typically, libidinal ego hope is dashed again and again, to be replaced by the angry, disappointed antilibidinal ego, which makes libidinal hope intolerably frustrating thus promoting its repression most of the time. The exciting object is a split-off fragment of the actual mother that retains its allure despite disappointing the child again and again. This ego structure is purely defensive, as it keeps the child emotionally attached to the mostly rejecting mother during the very worst periods of rejection and abandonment. The libidinal ego seems to be a fundamental human response to emotional starvation that has been overlooked by other models of psychoanalysis.

Clinically, it is *extremely inadvisable* to confront or even question the patient who is deeply immersed in this ego structure, as it indicates that they are desperately holding onto their needed objects as they have been threatened with abandonment, either in reality or in the consulting room. This sub-ego structure allows the child to keep hoping and eliminates the feeling that he/she has been abandoned.

Fairbairn's structures, as I have noted, appear in literature, memoirs and novels, as in the past quote by Katherine Anne Porter. The following example of a very powerful libidinal ego experience was written by Junot Diaz, a novelist and essayist for *New Yorker* magazine. His language conveys the intense need of a child for good objects. Diaz was born in Santo Domingo and by five years old had not met his father, who was in New York City. His neighbor got a television at this time, and he saw a Spider-Man cartoon with the following consequence.

A little context: I had a father in New York City whom I did not remember, and who (it was promised) would one day deliver my family to the States. And here was my first television and my first cartoon and my first superhero – a hero who was in America – and somehow it all came together for me in a lightning bolt of longing and imagination. My father's absence made perfect sense. He couldn't come back right away because he was fighting crime in N.Y.C. . . . as *Spider Man*. The diasporic imagination really is its own superpower.

(Diaz, 2017:42)

Diaz became a junior Spider-Man, climbing trees until he fell out of a tree and hurt himself badly. Then, a few years later, Diaz's father returned home and took his family to New Jersey, where he proved to be a major disappointment.

My father was the worst shock of all. He had no problem laying hands on us kids for the slightest infraction. Beating like he was making up for lost time. Like he was mad that he had a family. Before our first month was out, he had introduced my brother and me to his side chick as though it were the most normal thing in the world. It turns out that the old man did have a secret life in America, but it had nothing to do with fighting crime. No, he was not the hero I had dreamed of, and no amount of wishing could make it so. Are you surprised, then, that I was drawn back to the television? . . . Late into the night, when everyone else was asleep and almost no channels were on. Because I was lost, because I wanted help with my English, because my father was a nightmare. And because I was convinced, foolish little fantasist that I was, that somehow my family and I had ended up in the wrong America, and that the country and the father I'd first glimpsed on TV in Santo Domingo, the country and father I'd been promised, were still out there somewhere. Just had to find them. Never did.

(Diaz, 2017:42)

Few examples are as convincing as this one from Diaz regarding the power of the libidinal ego to provide the child with an object that he creates out of fantasy because he desperately needs help to grow and mature. Even when the reality of his father was an enormous disappointment, he went back to his libidinal ego fantasy that a good object father was somewhere to be found, because hope is essential for the individual to grow and develop.

All four of the sub-structures are "fanatics"; that is, they hold extreme positions of either love or hate, as illustrated by the Skolnick quote earlier. The stubborn resistance of the attachment between the antilibidinal ego and the rejecting object, and the equally intense relationship between the libidinal ego and the exciting object define Fairbairn's concept of "Attachment to Bad Objects". Odgen describes the ties between the two part-selves and their respective part objects in the following passage. Note that the ties between these internalized structures are one of the three major sources of resistance that will be discussed shortly.

> The libidinal nature of these ties suggests that aspects of the individual (the internal saboteur and the libidinal ego) have by no means given up on the potential of the unsatisfactory objects to give and receive love. It seems to me that a libidinal tie to an internal object towards whom one feels anger, resentment, and the like, necessarily involves an (unconscious) wish/need to use what control one feels one has to change the unloving and unaccepting (internal) object into a loving and accepting one. From this vantage point, I view the libidinal ego and the internal saboteur as aspects of self that are intent on transforming the exciting object and rejecting object into loving objects. Moreover, it seems to me, by extension of Fairbairn's thinking, that *the infant's effort to transform unsatisfactory objects into satisfactory objects – thus reversing the imagined toxic effect on the mother of the infant's love – is the single most important motivation sustaining the structure of the internal object world.* And that structure, when externalized, underlies all pathological external object relationships.

(Ogden, 2014:136)

This quote from Ogden may be the single best analysis of the motivation that sustains the inner world of so many patients. Their motivation is an extreme attempt to secure love from objects who simply have no love to give. Ogden's first statement that these ties (between the antilibidinal ego and the rejecting object and between the libidinal ego and the exciting object) are libidinal ties goes back to Suttie's earlier statement that hate is a complaint against not being loved by the object. It appears at first glance that the relationship between the antilibidinal ego and the rejecting object is based on hate, but a closer look informs us that the resentful attachment is based on anger from the child who is frustrated because the rejecting object has failed to love him. Ogden sees the whole motivation of human children (and later, adults) as being based on a strident insistence and demand that they be loved by the parent. In my experience, the motivation to change the bad object (either the critical side or the promising side) into a loving one was the baseline motivation in many of my adult patients' lives. The frustrated, enraged, yet still dependent antilibidinal ego complains, demands respect and undermines or otherwise harrasses the rejecting object in order to force it to acknowledge his/her value. This pressure from the antilibidinal ego toward the rejecting object is constant, and consists of an externalization of the internal dialogue between these related structures. In the following passage, Ogden describes the motivation of both the part self and the part object to maintain the status quo:

> The sub organization identified with the object (the rejecting part object) is under constant pressure from the self component (the antilibidinal ego) of the relationship to be transformed into a good object. Such a transformation is strenuously resisted by the object component, because this type of massive shift in identity would be experienced as an annihilation of an aspect of the ego. The internal object relationship is vigorously defended from two directions: The self-component is unwilling to risk annihilation resulting from absence of object relatedness and instead tries to change the bad object into a good one; at the same time the object component fends off annihilation that would result from being transformed into a new entity (the good object).
>
> (Ogden, 1990:157–158)

Ogden's perspective makes it clear that each component of both unconscious pairs needs the partner to "cooperate" with the other, and if they don't, both will perish, a point I have noted earlier.

As previously noted, any of the sub-egos or part objects can dominate the weakened, or never developed, central ego and take over the executive function. In the following passage, Scharff and Birtles describe a clinical scenario in which either one or the other of the part-self, part-object pairs can present in the clinical interview.

> Clinically we see patients who use anger to cover up the effect of unrequited longing stemming from their libidinal object constellation. They are more comfortable with an angry stance towards objects than with painfully unsatisfied longing. Although Fairbairn did not describe the parallel situation, once he pointed the way to the internal dynamic relationship between object relations sets, we

can see that the libidinal ego can also repress the anti-libidinal relationship, as represented in patients who show an exaggerated sense
of love and hope – a too-good-to-be-true personality – in order to
mask resentful anger that is even more painful to them.

(Scharff and Birtles, 2014:17)

Any of the four mostly unconscious structures can dominate the
patient's central ego during part or all of the clinical interview. Most
commonly the patient begins in his/her central ego, which may be soon
displaced by their antilibidinal ego, which can be focused either on the
original objects, or via transference on the analyst. This pattern prob-
ably compromises 75 or greater percent of the sessions. The next most
common pattern is for the patient to present in their libidinal ego, which
sees the analyst as the source of needed love and support. The two least
common presentations are the rejecting object patient, who is enraged
at being forced to seek treatment in the first place and is unsparing in
his/her aggression towards the analyst. This is a short-lived pattern, as
the patient almost always leaves. Finally, the least common pattern is
the patient who presents dominated by his/her exciting object structure
as someone who has untapped special talents and attempts to get the
analyst invested in their libidinal ego's hope for increased self love and
esteem if he/she is able to "cure" such a unique and special patient.

References

Beattie, H.J. (2005). Revenge. *Journal of the American Psychoanalytic Association*, 53 (2): 513–524.
Blizard, R. (2019). The role of double blinds, reality testing and
chronic relational trauma in the genesis and treatment of borderline
personality disorder. In Moskowitz, A., Dorahy, M., and Schafer, I.
Eds., *Psychosis, Trauma and Dissociation: Evolving Perspectives
on Severe Psychopathology*. Hoboken, NJ: John Wiley & Sons, pp.
367–380.
Bromberg, P. (1998). *Standing in the Spaces*. New York: Psychology
Press.
Celani, D.P. (2005). *Leaving Home: How to Separate from Your Dif-
ficult Family*. New York: Columbia University Press.
Celani, D.P. (2010). *Fairbairn's Object Relations in the Clinical Set-
ting*. New York: Columbia University Press.
Davies, J.M. (1996). "Linking the pre-analytic" with the postclassical.
Contemporary Psychoanalysis, 32 (4): 553–576.

Diaz, J. (2017). Waiting for Spider Man. *The New Yorker Magazine*, November 20.

Fairbairn, W.R.D. (1944). Endopsychic structure considered in terms of object relationships. In *Psychoanalytic Studies of the Personality*. London: Routledge & Kegan Paul, 1952, pp. 82–132.

Fairbairn, W.R.D. (1954). Observations on the nature of hysterical states. *British Journal of Medical Psychology*, 27: 105–125.

Mitchell, S.A. (1988). *Relational Concepts in Psychoanalysis, An Integration*. Cambridge, MA: Harvard University Press.

Mitchell, S.A. (2000). *Relationality: From Attachment to Intersubjectivity*. Hillsdale, NJ: The Analytic Press.

Odgen, T. (2010). Why read Fairbairn? In Clarke G. and Scharff, D. Eds., *Fairbairn and the Object Relations Tradition*. London, Karnac Books, pp. 131–146.

Ogden, T.H. (1990). *The Matrix of the Mind*. Northvale, NJ: Jason Aronson Inc.

Ogden, T.H. (2010). Why read Fairbairn? In Clarke, G. and Scharff, D.E. Eds., *Fairbairn and the Object Relations Tradition*. London: Karnac Books, 2014, pp. 249–262.

Porter, K.A. (1948). The necessary enemy. In *The Collected Essays and Occasional Writings of Katherine Anne Porter*. Boston: Houghton Mifflin, 1970.

Scharff, D.E. and Birtles, E.F. (1997). From instinct to self: The evolution and implications of W.R.D. Fairbairn's theory of object relations. In Clarke, G. and Scharff, D. Eds., *Fairbairn and the Object Relations Tradition*. London: Karnac Books, 2014, pp. 5–23.

Scharff, J. (2014). Self and society, trauma and the link. In Clarke, G. and Scharff, D., *Fairbairn and the Object Relations Tradition*. London: Karnac Books, pp. 365–377.

Skolnick, N.J. (2014). The analyst as a good object: A Fairbairnian perspective. In Clarke, G. and Scharff, D.E. Eds., *Fairbairn and the Object Relations Tradition*. London: Karnac, pp. 249–262.

Sutherland, J.D. (1989). *Fairbairn's Journey into the Interior*. London: Free Association Books.

Chapter 4

Preparing to Work Clinically With Fairbairn's Model

Errors Within the Structural Model

When working with Fairbairn's model, the clinician should be aware of aspects of the model that are not helpful, contradictory and/or do not follow the fundamental logic of the model. The largest problem in Fairbairn's model was his position on internalization of the good object, i.e. the parent that meets the infant and child's needs more or less continuously during their development. As mentioned previously, Fairbairn mistakenly assumed that internalization was a defensive procedure. This concept came from Klein's belief that the child's death instinct was so aggressive that the child's innate hate and envy of her mother would lead the child to lose the parent. To redress this eventuality, the infant was forced to internalize good objects from its relationship with the mother to counter the rage from the death instinct. Fairbairn repeated the idea that the internalization of good objects only occurred to buffer the toxic internalized bad objects (Fairbairn, 1943:66).

He discussed his belief that under ordinary circumstances, the child had no reason to internalize good objects. In the following quote, Fairbairn supports this faulty idea which appears in a long footnote in his 1944 paper.

> I should add that, in my opinion, it is always "bad" objects that are internalized in the first instance, since it's difficult to find any adequate motive for the internalization of objects which are satisfying and "good". Thus it would be a pointless procedure on the part of the infant to internalize the breast of a mother with whom he already had a perfect relationship in the absence of such

DOI: 10.4324/9781003394181-5

internalization, and whose milk proved sufficient to satisfy his incorporative needs. According to this line of thought it is only insofar as his mother's breast fails to satisfy his physical and emotional needs and thus becomes a bad object that it becomes necessary for the infant to internalize it. It is only later that good objects are internalized to defend the child's ego against bad objects which have been internalized already; and the superego is a "good-object" of this nature.

(Fairbairn, 1944:93)

Fairbairn added to this error by assuming the lack of internalization of good objects made the central ego (which is an ego structure) somehow different from the unconscious structures. That is, he assumed that the unconscious structures developed through internalization of one traumatic event after another, but positive experiences with objects in the external world *did not accumulate in exactly the same way*. This follows his false assumption that good objects were not internalized in the first place, except to buffer bad objects. This divergent pathway for the development of unconscious versus conscious structures *is simply inconsistent*. Within this model, both logic and consistency demand that all structures, whether built of loving supportive memories or of toxic trauma-inducing memories, have to accrue and develop in the same way. The more frequent the interaction (whether good or bad), the larger the pool of internalized memories which coalesce into powerful and influential structures. Fairbairn's ambivalence regarding the internalization of good objects has also been challenged and replaced by more current concepts. The most clear and straightforward solution to Fairbairn's ambivalence regarding internalization of good objects has been articulated by Scharff and Scharff (2000), who flatly state that Fairbairn made a mistake.

In Fairbairn's model, however, the introjection of good experience comes as a kind of afterthought: good objects are only introjected to compensate for bad (1952). Klein disagreed with Fairbairn's ideas that introjection of good experience was secondary. She thought that under the influence of the life instinct, good experience is also taken in from the beginning. Current infant research demonstrates that she was right, and all of us take in good and bad experiences. But we think that it happens, not because of the life and death instincts (as she thought), but simply because we are built to take in all kinds of experiences as we relate in order to grow as a person. The realities of all aspects of external experience and our perceptions of them provide the building blocks for our psychic structure.

(Scharff and Scharff, 2000:219–220)

The Scharff and Sharff quote eliminates the mistake that Fairbairn made. Additional support for the notion that Fairbairn made an error also comes from a clinical paper by Greenson (1971) that serves as a near-perfect counter-example to Fairbairn's position. Greenson described a military patient from when he was a military psychiatrist assigned to the Pacific Theater. He was responsible for the mental health of airmen who were traumatized from injuries and horrific experiences during the bombing of the Pacific Islands as the US worked its way toward the Japanese mainland. The loss of airmen was very high as bombers encountered anti-aircraft fire from the ground as well as from Japanese fighter planes. One bomber limped back to the base heavily damaged in both its airframe and mechanical systems from enemy fire, and surprisingly, six of the crew were alive and only the aerial photographer was assumed to have perished. He had been overwhelmed by caustic, hot gasoline from the many punctured fuel tanks and was trapped and drowning in the sealed bomb bay. When they opened the bomb bay, they discovered that the 19-year-old airman was still alive and rushed him to the hospital. During his recovery from skin burns, he told a nurse that he was hearing repeated verses of a simple song, "Amosnell, Domosnell, Amosnell, Domosnell" in his head, and he found them comforting. Greenson was called in by the nursing staff to investigate the possible meanings of these words. He consulted intelligence and they reported that the words were Flemish, from northern Belgium, and meant "I must hurry, You must hurry". The words were from a Flemish lullaby and meant "you must hurry" to sleep. He also asked his patient to write to his father and ask about his mother. The airman's father wrote and confirmed Greenson's suspicion that he had discovered an internalized good object.

Frank excitedly came to his session with a letter from his father. The father said that Frank's mother had died when he was not quite two years old: and that she had been born in Belgium and had come to the United States as a young girl. She had forgotten most of her mother tongue, but she would sing children's songs to Frank in

her native dialect when he was a baby. In fact, the father himself
recalled one that went something like "Amosnell Domosnell".

(Greenson, 1971:422)

This example strongly suggests that very early experiences with the
mother are internalized and stored in the central ego's unconscious,
which, when the child has a nurturing parent, is filled with good object
memories. The earliest memories may not be conscious, as they would
not be understood, but they add positive structure and comfort to the
central ego. As the child develops, these positive memories support
differentiation from the mother, and over time the child can separate
from her and venture into the external world.

Another major error in Fairbairn's original 1944 paper is related to
the prior error of the absence of internalization of good objects, and
it was the absence of an object partner for the central ego. The fundamental premise of Object Relations Theory is that every self has to
have either an external or internal object partner with whom to relate.
Fairbairn's diagram of his structural model (1952:105) has the central ego without a partner, because of his original, and clearly incorrect assumption, that internalization is a defensive maneuver, and thus
only frustrating objects (rejecting or exciting) were internalized. In the
diagram the central ego appears all alone, with no object with whom
to relate, and thus no object who supported or nurtured him/her during infancy and early development. I previously noted that Fairbairn
almost never revised his prior papers, with this one exception, which
was an Addendum (1951) modifying his earlier positions in his 1944
paper on structure. The Addendum was included in the 1952 publication of his collected papers. In this correction, Fairbairn added a
pathway for the good object to enter the individual's inner world and
act as an emotional support and parent for the central ego. These two
structures, the central ego and its "senior" partner, the Ideal or Idealized object, interact with each other and both remain conscious. They
remain conscious because the ideal object did not produce intolerable
frustration for the central ego during childhood, and thus it did not
produce intolerable relational memories from which the central ego
has to dissociate. The following quote from the Addendum illustrates
how Fairbairn allowed the ideal object to enter the child's inner world.

It will be noticed however, that, after the over-exciting and
over-frustrating elements have been split off from the internal

ambivalent object, there remains a nucleus of the object shorn of its over-exciting and over-rejecting elements. The nucleus will then assume the status of an "accepted object" in the eyes of the central ego, which will maintain the cathexis of this object and retain it for itself. . . . It will be noticed that, in accordance with my revised conception, the central ego's "accepted object", being shorn of its over-exciting and over rejecting elements, assumes the form of a desexualized and idealized object which the central ego can safely love.

(Fairbairn, 1951:135)

Thus the "ideal object" becomes a good internal object that can nurture, support and encourage the central ego and allow it to develop to its full potential. The description of this object as being "idealized" comes from the fact that the overly frustrating aspects of it have been split ("shorn" in Fairbairn's words) off. In nurturing families, very little idealization of the object is necessary as the good object parent who has met the child's needs most of the time, and has created little developmental frustration, would not require the child to use the splitting defense.

A second error, perhaps equally important, was Fairbairn's assumption that the central ego contained aggression and that its aggression was the force that kept the sub-egos repressed in the unconscious. Over time the structural model has been re-conceived as operating not on aggression between one pair of structures to another, but rather on anxiety. As mentioned previously, anxiety triggers one structure to emerge or conversely to retreat into the unconscious, for instance when the current dominant structure senses massive anxiety if it continues to remain in the dominant (executive) position.

Another problem in Fairbairn's model is that he formed his idea of the inner world of objects based on Freud's dynamic model and he had the different structures in his theory cross the dissociation barrier, as if they knew about each other. He also assumed that the antilibidinal ego could break free of its relational partner and attack the libidinal ego and its associated object, the exciting object. This is simply impossible given the rules inherent within the model. It is not possible, because the aggression between the antilibidinal ego and the rejecting object is completely encapsulated in their closed-off relationship and neither structure can break away from their relational partner. Secondly, the two pairs of structures are independent of each other and do not know about the other pair of structures.

Fairbairn made an *additional* related (and serious) mistake, in his assumption that the antilibidinal ego was the cooperative "enforcer" who did the bidding of the rejecting object, as noted in the following quote:

> But, meanwhile, my justification will be that the dreamer's mother, who provided the original model of this internalized object, was essentially a rejecting figure, and that it is, so to speak, in the name of this object that the aggression of the internal saboteur (antilibidinal ego) is directed against the libidinal ego.
>
> (Fairbairn, 1944:104)

As noted, the logic of Fairbairn's model does not allow one pair of structures to "know" about the other pair of structures. Fairbairn mistakenly assumed that the antilibidinal ego was a cooperative partner of the rejecting object, *which we now know is completely incorrect* – the two structures are implacable opponents and are focused completely on each other. The antilibidinal ego can't do the bidding of the rejecting object. Frankly, the section on internal dynamics is completely untenable.

When working with Fairbairn's structural model, these speculative, unobservable relationships are best left behind. We have to acknowledge the reality that Fairbairn was in the throes of a creative leap that offered a completely new vision of human psychological functioning. However, he was caught in his own time and was limited to the pre-existing energetic metaphors and by the classical model that had structures in a dynamic relationship to each other. Thus, in forming a whole new vision of the human personality, he was limited by the metaphors of his time, yet he still managed to create a completely different model of the human psyche.

The Three Sources of Resistance

The next issue for the clinician who intends to use Fairbairn's model for treatment is to understand the three major sources of resistance that emerge directly from his model. Each of the three different factors is distinct; these three forms of resistance can be seen in the consulting room and be identified as being separate from the others. All three forms of resistance are the result of the inner structures that have been developed in the patient's inner world. Fairbairn's views on resistance are the most integrated, consistent and understandable aspect of his model.

The first structural source of resistance comes directly from the dissociated memories that the patient has hidden from so he/she would not lose their attachment to their object. Fairbairn discusses this factor in the following beautifully worded passage from his 1943 paper:

> There is little doubt in my mind that, in conjunction with another factor to be mentioned later, the deepest source of resistance is fear of the release of bad objects from the unconscious; for, when such bad objects are released, the world around the patient becomes peopled with devils too terrifying for him to face . . . At the same time there is now little doubt in my mind that the release of bad objects from the unconscious is one of the chief aims which the psychotherapist should set himself out to achieve, even at the expense of a severe "transference neurosis"; for it is only when the internalized bad objects are released from the unconscious that there is any hope of their cathexis being dissolved. The bad objects can only be safely released, however, if the analyst has become established as a sufficiently good object for the patient. Otherwise the resulting insecurity may prove insupportable.
>
> (Fairbairn, 1943:69)

This is one of the best quotes from Fairbairn, and it emerges directly from his theory of dissociated bad objects that challenge the central ego's view of reality. Fairbairn uses the words "release" or "released" five times in this short passage. He is referring to the ability of a patient to describe, from his/her central ego's perspective, what happened to him/her in childhood as opposed to holding it away from consciousness in a repressed structure. It often takes months of treatment before the traumatic events can be approached, and then slowly at best. When a patient begins to realize how traumatic and unloving his personal history was, he must have a reliable supportive object to join him/her and validate the memory as well as support them, as the patient has now lost trust in their original objects and their sense of being grounded in their family. Ideally, the patient may eventually be able to recognize that they have been living in an illusionary family, one that they constructed to save themselves from absolute abandonment, and the process of discovery can take several years.

The second source of structural resistance, which Fairbairn alluded to in the previous quote, is the attachment between the libidinal ego and the exciting object, and the attachment between the antilibidinal ego and the rejecting object which he addressed in his 1944 paper, and which was discussed previously. This second source of resistance emerges both from the attachment of the libidinal ego's desperate need for love from their exciting object, and the equally powerful attachment of the antilibidinal ego's aggression and resentment directed toward the rejecting object. Fairbairn's statements about this source of resistance in the following passage are clear and to the point.

> In terms of my present standpoint, there can be no room for doubt that the obstinate attachment of the libidinal ego to the exciting object and its reluctance to renounce this object constitute a particularly formidable source of resistance – and one that plays no small part in determining what is known as the negative therapeutic reaction. . . . The truth is that, however well the fact may be disguised, the individual is extremely reluctant to abandon his original hate, no less than his original need, of his original objects in childhood.
>
> (Fairbairn, 1944:117)

These internal structures support the abused, ignored or neglected child because each part-ego gives the child hope that he/she will either be recognized by the rejecting object as a valuable person, or he/she will be finally loved by the exciting object. This never-accomplished goal is one of the factors in the individual's inability to differentiate and begin a new life of their own. These two powerful structures in the internal world keep the individual fully occupied. As noted previously, the libidinal ego's determination not to give up hope of being loved and its refusal to let go of the exciting object whose "promise" has sustained him/her over time appears, at first glance, to be the more formidable source of resistance. However, it is equally difficult for the antilibidinal ego to let go of its determination to reform the rejecting object who in the past stripped him of his dignity, humiliated him, and filled his inner world with hundreds of accusations of badness and failure that he has internalized. These are the two fundamental motivations of the individual's two sub-egos. These motivations preoccupy the individual and make success in the external world no longer feasible, because of the individual's inability to differentiate from his parental objects and engage fully with external objects.

The third source of resistance, and one that also comes directly from the model, is from the projection of inner templates of objects onto objects in the external world – in a word, transference. The internalized structures have extreme views of reality, and are uncompromising. They resist input from external objects, and in fact, they misperceive external objects and transform them into new individuals that mimic the attitudes of the patient's internal objects. The inner world is a fortress of safety and partial satisfactions, and is the only world in which the schizoid feels comfortable and safe. Fairbairn saw that projection of the individual's inner world into outer reality was the fundamental source of transference.

Insofar as the inner world assumes the form of a closed system, a relationship with an external object is only possible in terms of transference, viz. on condition that the external object is treated as an object within the closed system of inner reality.

(Fairbairn, 1958:381)

Fairbairn also saw the fundamental dynamic between the patient and the analyst as a struggle in which the patient attempts to include his analyst into a familiar role as an internal object, and conversely the analyst struggles to be seen as an external object, free of patient projections.

Thus, in a sense, psycho-analytical treatment resolves itself into a struggle on the part of the patient to press-gang his relationship with the analyst into the closed system of the inner world through the agency of transference, and a determination on the part of the analyst to effect a breach in this closed system and provide conditions under which, in the setting of a therapeutic relationship, the patient may be induced to accept the open system of outer reality.

(Fairbairn, 1958:385)

Regardless of the warmth, honesty and sincerity of the analyst, the patient will mistake him/her for one of the established inner characters from his early experience in his family. This misperception can, if severe, halt all progress as the analyst is experienced by the patient as someone completely at odds with the reality of the analyst. Fairbairn's assessment of this form of structural resistance is that it is "colossal", as noted in the following quote taken from his 1958 paper.

> I consider the term "analysis" as a description of psycho-analytical treatment is really a misnomer, and that *the chief aim of psycho-analytical treatment is to promote a maximum "synthesis" of the structures into which the original ego has been split, in the setting of a therapeutic relationship with the analyst. . . .* The resistance on the part of the patient to the achievement of these aims, is of course, colossal; for he has a vested interest in maintaining his the early split of his internalized object, upon which, according to my theory, the split of his ego depends, and which represents a defense against the dilemma of ambivalence. . . . Implied in these various manifestations of resistance on the part of the patient is a further defensive aim which I have now come to regard *as the greatest of all sources of resistance-viz. the maintenance of the patient's internal world as a closed system.* In terms of the theory the mental constitution which I have proposed, the maintenance of such a closed system involves the perpetuation of the relationships prevailing between the various ego structures and their respective internal objects, as well as between one another; and since the nature of these relationships is the ultimate source of both symptoms and deviations of character, *it becomes still another aim of psycho-analytical treatment to effect breaches of the closed system which constitutes the patient's inner world, and thus make his world accessible to the influence of outer reality.*
>
> (Fairbairn, 1958:380)

This is an enormously insightful quote from Fairbairn as it addresses both the aims of analytic treatment and one of the sources of resistance that opposes the analyst's efforts. It also springs directly from the core of his model. Fairbairn's language underemphasizes the importance of the patient's motivation to avoid "the dilemma of ambivalence". It would be more accurate to describe the consequences of integration as the annihilation of the patient's sense of self, of having a particular identity, of being a member of a specific family, and of having lost the most important connections to others in the world.

Fairbairn had the correct analysis of patient resistance but left no instructions for the practitioner of his model. The patient's defenses are all constructed to prevent a breach of their inner world, but no strategy is offered. If such a breach is prematurely accomplished and actually takes place, then the entire defensive structure, which is designed to *prevent* reality from intruding, would collapse, which would then plunge the patient into an abandonment crisis.

The Goals of Psychoanalytic Treatment Informed by Fairbairn's Model

The following quote from Fairbairn's 1958 paper on treatment announced his position regarding the importance of the relationship between the patient and the analyst. Once again, Fairbairn ignored the conventional wisdom of psychoanalysis of his day with its emphasis on interpretation, and replaced it with the non-analytic concept of the interpersonal impact of an object in external reality as an agent of change of the patient's inner world, which also acts as a stimulus for restarting the stalled emotional development.

It becomes obvious, therefore, that, from a therapeutic standpoint, interpretation is not enough; and it would appear to follow that the relationship existing between the patient and the analyst in the psychoanalytical situation serves purposes additional to that of providing a setting for the interpretation of transference phenomena. In terms of the object-relations theory of the personality, the disabilities from which the patient suffers represents the effects of unsatisfactory and unsatisfying object-relationships experienced in early life and perpetuated in an exaggerated form in inner reality; and, if this view is correct, the actual relationship existing between the patient and the analyst as a person must be regarded as in itself constituting a therapeutic factor of prime importance. The existence of such a personal relationship in outer reality not only serves the function of providing a means of correcting the distorted relationships which prevail inner reality and influence the reactions of the patient to outer objects, but provides the patient an opportunity, denied to him in childhood, to undergo a process of emotional development in the setting of an actual relationship with a reliable and beneficent parental figure.

(1958:377)

As established in the earlier chapters, psychopathology from the object relation's perspective is the consequence of the child or young adult protecting himself/herself from both finding out how badly he has been/is being treated, which prevents both differentiation and integration, and so the concept of the analyst aiding emotional development, which was thwarted by the original objects, is completely consistent with the model.

Fairbairn had a theoretically clear view of the goals of treatment, and he used a territorial metaphor to describe the fundamental goal in the first quote:

> From the topographic standpoint, it must be regarded as relatively immutable, although I conceive it as one of the chief aims of psychoanalytical therapy to introduce some change into its topography by way of a territorial adjustment. Thus I conceive it as among the most important functions of psychoanalytical therapy (a) to reduce the split of the original ego by restoring to the central ego a maximum of the territories ceded to the libidinal ego and the internal saboteur, and (b) to bring the exciting object and the rejecting object as far as possible together within the sphere of influence of the central ego.
>
> (Fairbairn, 1944:130)

This quote describes the analytic task of increasing the power of the central ego to be able to tolerate dissociated parts of experience that had to be split off, and Chapter Five will describe a technique designed to accomplish this goal.

Fairbairn then follows with a second quote describing a parallel process to the first, which is to help the patient identify his internal bad objects and specify why they are bad (frustrating to the patient's developmental needs). Treatment simultaneously offers the patient an alternative good object as a replacement for the bad objects. This process begins when the analyst carefully examines apparently insignificant events from the patient's childhood and attributes motivation to the parent who created the toxic event. This second part of treatment cannot begin until the patient has recognized and accepted the analyst as a partner and not as a destructive enemy out to destroy their family.

> It follows from what precedes that among the various aims analytical technique should be 1) to enable the patient to release from his unconscious "buried" bad objects which have been internalized

and repressed because originally they seemed intolerable, and (2) to provide a dissolution of the libidinal bonds whereby the patient is attached to these hitherto indispensable bad objects.

(Fairbairn, 1944:74)

Once again, Fairbairn was able to articulate just what needed to be done; however, he failed to give the reader/student specific guidance (or any guidance at all) on how to accomplish the desired goal. He did note in passing that a relationship with a person who is a good object is an "indispensable factor" in separating the patient from his bad objects;

The moral would seem to be that the appeal of a good object is an indispensable factor in promoting a dissolution of the cathexis of internalized bad object, and that the significance of the transference situation is partly derived from this fact.

(Fairbairn, 1943:74)

However, Fairbairn never gave the reader instructions as to what the good object should do. The following quote from Ogden (2014) expands upon Fairbairn's view of treatment in which the goal is to introduce the central ego to split off aspects of himself that have been up to now completely unacceptable to the central ego, in a way that is tolerable.

Psychological growth, for Fairbairn (as I read him), involves a form of acceptance of oneself that can be achieved only in the context of a real relationship with a relatively psychologically mature person. A relationship of this sort (including the analytic relationship) is the only possible exit from the solipsistic world of internal object relationships. Self-acceptance is a state of mind that marks the (never fully achieved) relinquishment of the life consuming effort to transform unsatisfactory internal object relationships into satisfactory (i.e., loving and accepting) ones. With psychological growth one comes to know at a depth that one's early experience with one's unloving and unaccepting mother will never be other than what they were. It is a waste of time to devote oneself to the effort to transform oneself (and others) into people one wishes one were (or wishes they were). In order to take part in experience in a world populated by people whom one has not invented, and from whom one may learn, the individual must first loosen the unconscious bonds of resentment, addictive love, contempt, and disillusionment that confine him to a life lived principally in the mind.

(Ogden, 2014:144)

Ogden is brusque and bold in his view of the damage done to the individual by his/her "fixation" on the objects that caused the damage to their personality development: "It is a waste of time to devote oneself to the effort to transform oneself (and others) into people one wishes one were (or wishes they were)". From a developmental perspective, the individual's focus on the inner world and internal objects simply delays maturity of the self as well as interfering with the processes of differentiation and integration. The essential factor is a supportive relationship with an analyst who is able to titrate the quantity and severity of dissociated memories that he/she explores cooperatively with the patient. The analytic environment must be structured and supportive enough that the patient borrows and slowly internalizes the ego strength that he/she sees in the analyst, which allows him/her to experience the painful and confusing dissociated thoughts or self-presentations in the presence of a good object. Fairbairn addressed exactly this issue in the following quote.

The bad objects can only be safely released however, if the analyst has become established as a sufficiently good object for the patient. Otherwise the resulting insecurity may prove insupportable.

(Fairbairn, 1943:40)

The relational perspective assumes that all the patient's productions are fragments of the patient's self in relation to the part objects that were internalized during any number of developmental traumas that had to be dissociated during childhood. The analyst's calm and thoughtful responses to the surprising, if not frightening, patient productions can then be internalized by the patient. In effect, when the analyst says, "what an interesting part of you just appeared in this office", the patient gradually learns to reduce his/her fear of split-off aspects of himself/herself that previously seemed like the onset of madness. The task of separating any given patient from his current bad objects can be exceedingly difficult because of the activity of the internalized structures. As mentioned, these structures contain powerful motivations either to find or force love out of the exciting object or to confront and defeat the rejecting object's attack on the antilibidinal ego. Mitchell (1988) has written about the difficulties of this task because the patient is not simply a passive "container" of bad objects, but rather one who seeks out and actively pursues bad objects because they match the templates of their faulty parents lodged in their inner worlds.

> Psychopathology often entails an active, willful clinging to, an insistence on maladaptive relational patterns, symptomatic behaviors, and painful experiences. . . . Let me briefly note the importance of active commitment in Fairbairn's object-relations theory, which is somewhat different from a more purely developmental arrest position. Fairbairn argues that beneath all forms of psychopathology one finds an attachment to "bad objects" thereby pointing to an active dimension which Guntrip's later formulation loses. . . . We often observe not just the avoidance of the positive, but a fascination with the negative. Analysands with repetitive disturbances in interpersonal relations are drawn, like the moth to the flame, to specific negative types of relations-with sadistic, skittish, withdrawn, debilitated others. This compulsive repetition of painful early experience seems to reflect a detachment from some forms of relationship, and also an attachment to certain others. The masochistic character seeks abuse partially because the violence imparts a fantasy of connection with a schizoid or depressed parent, so unavailable in other ways. . . . Psychopathology is not a state of aborted, frozen development, but a cocoon actively woven of fantasized attachment to significant others. Beneath a seemingly passive detachment is often a secret attachment, largely unconscious, but experienced as necessary and life sustaining.
>
> (Mitchell, 1988:162–163)

Mitchell's point is that the struggle between patient, who defends his internalized bad objects ferociously, and the analyst can be prolonged and emotional, with the patient fighting to retain his attachments to objects that have given his life meaning and purpose. In the final chapter, we will take up the issue of creating and maintaining a clinical narrative that allows dissociated material to emerge, be understood and be remembered by the patient as important development factors in his/her personal history.

References

Fairbairn, W.R.D. (1941). A revised psychopathology of the psychoses and psychoneuroses. In *Psychoanalytic Studies of the Personality*. London: Routledge & Kegan Paul, 1952, pp. 28–58.

Fairbairn, W.R.D. (1943). The repression and return of bad objects (with special references to the "war neuroses"). In *Psychoanalytic Studies of the Personality*. London: Routledge & Kegan Paul, 1952, pp. 59–81.

Fairbairn, W.R.D. (1944). Endopsychic structure considered in terms of object relationships. In *Psychoanalytic Studies of the Personality*. London: Routledge & Kegan Paul, 1952, pp. 82–132.

Fairbairn, W.R.D. (1951). Addendum. In *Psychoanalytic Studies of the Personality*. London: Routledge & Kegan Paul, pp. 133–136.

Fairbairn, W.R.D. (1952). *Psychoanalytic Studies of the Personality*. London: Routledge & Kegan Paul.

Fairbairn, W.R.D. (1958). On the nature and aims of psycho-analytical treatment. *International Journal of Psychoanalysis*, 39: 374–385.

Greenson, R.R. (1971). A dream while drowning. In *Explorations in Psychoanalysis*. Madison, CT: International Universities Press, 1978, pp. 415–423.

Mitchell, S.A. (1988). *Relational Concepts in Psychoanalysis: An Integration*. Cambridge, MA: Harvard University Press.

Ogden, T.H. (2010). Why read Fairbairn? In Clarke, G. and Scharff, D.E. Eds., *Fairbairn and the Object Relations Tradition*. London: Karnac, 2014, pp. 249–262.

Scharff, J.S. and Scharff, D.E. (2000). *Object Relations Individual Therapy*. Northvale, NJ: Jason Aronson.

Chapter 5

Working With Fairbairn's Model in the Clinical Setting

Davies (1998) has written one of the best relational descriptions of the analytic dyad, in which she uses a "theater" metaphor to describe the interaction between the analyst and patient. Her description includes the unconscious structures possessed by the analyst that are called into a relationship with the cooperating member of the patient's unconscious structure. Thus, when using Fairbairn's internal structures, her description sees that the patient's antilibidinal ego activates the analyst's rejecting object, though what the analyst actually does when confronted with the patient's antilibidinal ego is based on the model with which he/she is working. Similarly, when the patient's libidinal ego emerges, the analyst's exciting object structure is invited to engage, and once again, the analyst's response depends on the model he/she is using.

> For contemporary relational analysts the transference countertransference matrix, as co constructed by patient and analyst becomes the transitional stage on which the Fairbairnian cast of characters, in ongoing improvisional interaction with the analyst's complementary troupe of players, can through projective identification and other projective-introjective mechanisms, begin to tell the story of "multiple selves in interaction". Such character driven dramas as those which unfold in the tapestry of interactive dialogues between the patient and therapist become the substance of a new psychoanalytic agenda. The drama progresses scene by scene, by dint of what we have come to call enactments, that is the personified embodiments of relationally derived unconscious fantasies as they force themselves outward onto the interpersonally receptive medium of the transference-countertransference experience.
>
> (Davies, 1998:67)

DOI: 10.4324/9781003394181-6

This description gives equal weight to both participants in the relationship. The real issue is how the analyst responds to the "invitations to react" from either hostile passive aggressive statements coming from the patient's antilibidinal ego structure, or alternatively, the excessive hope and the idealization of the analyst expressed by the patient's libidinal structure.

I will use a colorful example reported by Searles (1965) as an example of Davies' metaphor of the unfolding of a play, along with analysis of the interactions using Fairbairn's structural model to illustrate how this model can be used to understand interpersonal interactions that occur in the clinical interview. Searles is exceedingly generous with clinical descriptions in his writing. In the following passage, he describes a schizophrenic patient who had been hospitalized for ten years and had a number of previous therapists. This patient would enter Searles' office, sit slumped down in a chair, dropping cigarette ashes on the floor, picking his nose and passing flatus, which is the most extreme antilibidinal stance that I have ever encountered in the literature. The patient's antilibidinal stance was designed to provoke rage, aggression and counter-contempt from Searles. This behavior in any other setting, would likely succeed in provoking the rejecting object structure in a less experienced psychiatrist to emerge and clash with the patient's antilibidinal structure. In this example, the patient's antilibidinal sub-ego attempts to undermine Searles' authority and power, but the inherent dependency within the patient's structure prevents him from doing anything that would get him completely rejected, so he stays just inside the line of "acceptability".

> For about two and a half years his behavior during my sessions with him was limited almost exclusively to (a) sitting in a slovenly torpor, dropping cigarette ash on my rug, picking his nose and wiping the yield therefrom upon his trousers, and making no sound except for belches and the extremely frequent and quite unrepentant loud passage of flatus; and (b) infrequent vitriolic outbursts at me, in which he would give every evidence of being barely able to restrain himself from attacking me physically, and would say things as "You black, slimy son of a bitch! Shut up or I'll knock your teeth out!" As the months wore on I felt under increasing strain because of his massive resistance to psychotherapy, and increasingly afraid of his tenuously-controlled rage.

(Searles, 1965:201)

Fairbairn's model would suggest that this patient's sudden shift from a passive-aggressive display of contempt to an outburst of violent threats is the result of a sudden shift in ego states from an extreme antilibidinal part self to its unconscious partner – the enraged rejecting object. The outburst from the rejecting object is extremely aggressive because this structure is not dependent on any external object as it believes its rigid and hostile views are absolutely correct, a perfect internalization of the erstwhile rejecting parent. Thus the rejecting object does not fear being forced to leave the therapeutic relationship, or any other relationship for that matter. Searles speculated that his patient had picked up his (Searles') contempt for him and was responding with threats of violence because of what Searles was saying nonverbally.

Fairbairn's structural theory offers a *completely* different hypothesis. As noted, the patient's initial passive, hostile and contemptuous behavior is assumed to originate in the patient's antilibidinal ego. The patient's behavior communicates that he is angry at Searles for being forced to come to his office and consequently wants to offend Searles as much as possible, (without being expelled from the office or the institution). Fairbairn's model assumes that the patient's antilibidinal ego was attempting to engage the rejecting part object in Searles. When the patient suddenly switches to an aggressive verbal attack on Searles, the Fairbairnian model assumes that the attack originated in the rejecting object structure. This sudden shift from one structure to its dissociated partner may have originated with the patient's shifting view of Searles. At the outset of each session, Searles might have been experienced as a powerful rejecting object who had the power to summon the angry, unwilling patient to his office for a session, clearly against the patient's will. When the patient's extreme antilibidinal display of contempt did not engage Searles' rejecting object structure and he remained available and did nothing to retaliate against the patient, the patient's enraged but intimidated antilibidinal ego became emboldened because Searles appeared to be weak. Given this perception on the patient's part, his antilibidinal ego was repressed and replaced by his rejecting object structure, which now had a "weak" target upon whom to discharge internalized rage from his childhood. This shift in ego states was not based on anxiety, which is more common, but rather on the opportunity afforded to the rejecting object structure by the therapeutic environment. Fairbairn's model would have predicted that a patient with such an extreme antilibidinal ego would have had to experience vicious, violent and terrifying levels of abuse in childhood, which in turn would have been internalized and become an equally intense rejecting object structure in his inner world, which now discharged its violent threats on Searles. In the next example we can see the reverse scenario, where a patient's rejecting object attack activated the analyst's antilibidinal structure.

If we return to Davies' description of treatment as the unfolding of a play in which each of the characters meets the other's substructures and responds to the invitation to interact, we can understand the dynamics of the following encounter between Skolnick (2014) and a long-term patient. He gives us a wonderfully clear description of his own antilibidinal structure that was provoked by his patient's rejecting object tirade. His antilibidinal response was imagined but was not expressed. Skolnick had replaced the patient chair in his office while this particular patient was on vacation, without warning her about the change before she left. The patient was enraged by this sudden disruption of the framework and became dominated by her rejecting part object structure, which launched an aggressive tirade against Skolnick. Her rejecting object engaged his antilibidinal response, which he described in the following manner.

> When Marianna precipitously attacked, I was unprepared. Unwittingly I experienced and displayed a measure of stunned disturbance. She observed my discomfort, which in the moment I neither went to great length lengths to express nor hide. My unsettling and shameful sadistic impulses bubbled up fueling an inner and pleasurably charged string of invectives. My internal voice gleefully, though guiltily, complained, "I can't just buy a fucking chair without you giving me grief," and the like. Continuing to curse to myself, I pressed my imaginary eject button and pleasurably watched her fly out the window, sail uncontrollably over Central Park, and land in a strong icy current of the East River. I was now, in an experience paralleling hers, getting pleasure from my fantasized sadistic attack.
>
> (Skolnick, 2014:257)

This example illustrates just how enraged many adults are at events in their childhoods that offended them but had no voice to complain, and thus their rage was dissociated into their antilibidinal egos, which now emerge in the transference via their rejecting object structure. Skolnick's response is a candid and creative description of his own antilibidinal ego, hidden from others and working in fantasy to retaliate against a rejecting object patient who was undermining and attacking him, and one to whom he could not express his counter-aggression interpersonally.

Creating a Clinical Narrative that Disrupts the Relationship Between the Inner Structures

The model of treatment that I will offer, informed by Fairbairn's model, emerges directly from his writings. The overall approach is most similar to that described by Schafer (1998), who described the analytic relationship as a series of telling and retelling of life stories. Schafer acknowledges that there are many differing points of view and describes the variations between models with the concept of "narrativity of knowledge", which assumes that each therapeutic dyad, with an analyst or therapist of any given theoretical persuasion, will create a reasonable and agreed-upon (between the patient and analyst) understanding of the patient's developmental history.

> According to this point of view, the clinical psychoanalytic dialogue is best understood as a series of tellings and retellings by both parties to the dialogue. In addition the interpretive lines followed by the analyst in his or her interventions and increasingly accepted, assimilated and used by the analysand may be understood as derived from master narratives. These master narratives make up the so called general theory and major concepts of the analysts school of psychoanalytic thought. The analyst's detailed interpretive efforts may then be regarded as story lines that are manifestations of these master narratives.
>
> (Schafer, 1998:239)

Thus, when using Fairbairn's model as the master narrative, the analyst retells the patient's description of any given event that the patient reports with the addition of comments, often focusing on the emotional impact that the parent's behavior may have had on his/her patient in terms feelings of abandonment or of personal insult. This sets up a co-created dialogue where the patient can agree or disagree with the analyst's comments. In an earlier publication, Schafer notes that the tellings and retellings of the patient's story are not an exact replica of what the patient experienced in childhood, but rather a continuously evolving retelling that eventually creates a close approximation of what happened in childhood:

> It is especially important to emphasize that narrative is not an alternative to truth or reality: rather, it is the mode in which inevitable truth and reality are presented. We have only versions of the true and the real. . . . Psychoanalysis is conducted as a dialogue. . . . In this dialogue actions and happenings (for example traumatic events) are continuously being told by the analysand. Closure is always provisional to allow for further retellings. . . . Often the analysand responses to the analyst's intervention are themselves regarded as material to be retold (clarified, interpreted) in order to progress toward insight. Insight itself refers to those retellings that make a beneficial difference in a person's construction and reconstruction of experience and adaptively active conduct of life. Each retelling amounts to an account of the prior telling as something different or, more likely, something more that had been noted previously. In this dialogic way, each analysis amounts in the end to retelling a life in the past and present – and as it may be in the future. A life is re-authored as it is co-authored.
>
> (Schafer, 1992:xiv–xv)

Thus, the narrative becomes more refined and accurate over the many retellings. When setting up a Fairbairnian informed narrative with a patient, the analyst is directing the conversation to specific areas, namely the patient's splitting of objects and the unearthing of dissociated events that are buried in the patient's unconscious. A typical Fairbairnian informed narrative begins by focusing on apparently minor traumas from parental failures that the patient can verbalize at the outset of treatment.

The clinical narrative is designed to reduce the splits in the central ego by making the dissociated structures more accessible to it, while simultaneously decreasing the fantasies about the rejecting object and the exciting object in the inner world. At the outset of treatment, it was quite common for my patients to tell me that they forgot most of what we discussed by the time they walked to their car. As the central ego's strength increases it will be able to remember negative memories contained in the unconscious structures that the patient had previously found to be toxic. This approach relies on gently repeating the truths that the patient tells the analyst before they fully understand the implications of these stories to their development. Over time, the alliance between the central egos of both the patient and the analyst will contain those truths from session to session. As Fairbairn said, the patient's resistance will be "colossal", and he illustrated the problem of the patient's unearthing bad object memories in the following quote.

> Paradoxically enough, if it is an aim of analytical technique to promote a release of repressed bad objects from the unconscious, it is also fear of just such a release that characteristically drives the patient to seek analytical aid in the first instance. It is true that it is from his symptoms that he consciously desires to be relieved, and that a considerable proportion of psychopathological symptoms consist essentially in defenses against a "return of the repressed" (i.e. a return of repressed objects). Nevertheless, it is usually when his defenses are wearing thin and proving inadequate to safeguard him against anxiety over a threatened release of bad objects that he is driven to seek analytical aid. From the patient's point of view, accordingly, the effect of analytical treatment is to promote the very situation from which he seeks to escape.
>
> (Fairbairn, 1943:75)

As Fairbairn has just noted, the analyst is quietly instigating a discussion that is toxic to the patient, i.e., "to promote the very situation from which he seeks to escape"; however, in this retelling of his story there is a major difference, which is the presence of an interested, attentive and empathic "other". The focus of this approach is to make the discussion of the rejecting object a quiet center of treatment that is constantly present but is done subtly and without fanfare. This approach is designed to gradually dissolve the illusions and idealizations of the antilibidinal ego about the rejecting object until it completely loses its relevance as a significant object. It also explores the painful rejections that have been hidden under a blanket of denial, excuses, or outright dissociation. This process occurs simultaneously with the patient's use of the analyst's views of him/her to slowly create a modified sense of self that is independent of the originally toxic view of themselves that came from their parents' opinions of and treatment of them.

This approach will still run into resistance (all three that were mentioned), the most obvious one being the intensification of libidinal ego-based resistance to the analyst's positions on the failures of the patient's parents. The analyst must be prepared to temporarily abandon aspects of inquiry, particularly at the outset of treatment when the patient senses threats of abandonment as they are describing their history. During the process, the patient may split back to his/her libidinal view of their objects as being exciting and containing love. If this happens, it is unwise and counterproductive to contradict the patient or challenge their libidinal view of their objects. The patient's retreat to his/her libidinal ego signals that they are in great distress, and their central ego is unable to tolerate any more information about their developmental history. This holds true even when the patient begins (or continues) a self-destructive relationship with an abusive object, up to the point where real physical danger is present.

The patient's central ego will gain strength from the analyst's calm acceptance of what happened to their patient developmentally, which makes those events understandable to the patient's central ego. The presence of the analyst as a new object, around which the patient can gradually construct a new version of themselves, is the key component to the process. The new vision of their childhood, as well as of themselves, as mediated by an increasingly significant attachment to a new good object, allows the patient's central ego to tolerate new information about the rejecting object without plunging him/her into an abandonment crisis or being flooded by chaotic emotionality, as Bromberg (1998) notes in the following quote. Again in this quote, Bromberg focuses on the flooding of affect that threatens to disable the central ego, as opposed to Fairbairn's emphasis on the existential dread of abandonment.

That is, treatment has to gradually diminish a patient's vulnerability to feeling traumatized by input from any source that signals the potential threat of flooding him with unregulatable hyperarousal. Put another way, the core analytic goal is to always keep in mind is to facilitate a safe reorganization of self-structure into one that is stable and sturdy enough to withstand the input from another person's mind without it triggering the shadow of early trauma. As long as he remains unable to deal with the mind off an other without dread of retraumatization, then he has no choice but to rely on the dissociative "truths" held by each of his unbridgeable self-states in order to keep the other's subjectivity from overwhelming his own experience of selfhood.

(Bromberg, 1998:302–303)

At the outset of the narrative, very little can be said as the relationship between the analyst and the patient's central ego has yet to be established, and only then can the topic of parental failures be approached. I encountered a number of female patients who were lacking in trust and would "reframe" virtually everything that I said in the language of "Chakras", which was a clear signal to me that they were not going to accept my input, and so the relationships between myself and these patients were not successfully established. Another patient consulted me because her seven-month marriage had not been consummated. She could not accept any cooperative alliance with me and left after the second session, saying that I looked too concerned as she spoke and that I took her history too seriously, despite the fact that I had only been listening and had not made a single comment. My assumption was that she was completely unprepared to tolerate any new information regarding her developmental history. Finally, a middle-aged, socially isolated man came to me for a consultation and whenever I tried to speak, he would wave his hands in front of his chest, as if he was signaling an oncoming car. His message was that he didn't want to hear anything from me.

I would begin my narrative by asking for a retelling of my patient's developmental history and would just say "really" with slight surprise in my voice when the patient would relate an apparently minor childhood event that showed lack of empathy or aggression toward them without commenting further. If the patient asked what I meant, I would minimize my response and say that it sounded a bit unusual to me, for instance, that a parent would furiously throw his/her child's ice cream cone out of the window of a car when the child was unable to eat it fast enough to keep from dripping. To say too much, or emphasize the object's "badness" too forcefully, will hinder if not stop the process and cause the patient to become increasingly defensive. The level of defensive sensitivity is a good measure of the patient's need to remain attached to their objects. When applying this strategy, I would explain Fairbairn's concepts on dependency and developmental needs in the most general way to avoid appearing to speak down to the patient. Later on in treatment I would never use the concept of splitting, but instead would say that my patient was "of two minds" about their parents. I also was careful to keep track of shifts in my patient's ego states, particularly how much tolerance they had to hear my initial views regarding their family's level of empathy toward them before they would split into their libidinal ego for safety and relief. I found that knowing which ego structure you are dealing with at any given point in the dialogue is a key skill of the clinician who uses Fairbairn's structural model, as (for instance) it reveals just how strong the central ego is, and how quickly the libidinal ego emerges to protect the patient from unwanted discussions. For instance, when any of my patients became overwhelmed by the intensity of parental rejection they heard in the material *that they themselves were relating*, I would try and prevent them from splitting into their libidinal ego by immediately back-pedaling and suggesting that we stop digging so deeply into their history, often saying "There is good in everyone". I found that this would break the tension and the patient would be relieved as they valued the opportunity to tell their story to a careful listener who believed them (often for the first time in their life), without simultaneously being troubled and defensive by my generally negative assessment of their early childhood. By backing away, the patient could retain my attention and presence, without constantly defending the goodness of their still-necessary objects. I was always surprised at how "forgiving" my patients were toward me in these instances, as they wanted the relationship with me to continue while simultaneously retaining their attachment to their still-needed objects.

This approach is based on Fairbairn's structural theory in which the analyst allies himself/herself with the central ego during those times when it is available, and at other times he/she allies himself/herself with the patient's antilibidinal ego. This is the pathway to create a "breach" in the patient's inner world. The analyst listens to the patient's antilibidinal complaints and notes, for instance, that the patient might be trying to convince his rejecting object that he/she is a worthy person, when in fact work with the client has revealed that the rejecting object parent has never paid attention to him, nor to other members of the family, and perhaps is so self-centered that he/she hardly knows of other people's existence. In essence, the analyst undermines the patient's idealization, as well as the importance, power, and status, of the rejecting object. As angry and bitter as the antilibidinal ego is toward the rejecting object, this unconscious structure still sees the rejecting object as a legitimate authority that must be convinced of his/her goodness. Fairbairn noted this point in the following quote, in which he observed that bad internalized objects retain their "prestige" in the inner world: "But in attempting to control them in this way, he is internalizing objects which have wielded power over him in the external world: and these objects retain their prestige for power over him in the inner world" (Fairbairn, 1943:67).

Over time, the analyst carefully and deliberately undermines the "prestige" that the patient's antilibidinal ego feels for the rejecting object. In the process, the patient's antilibidinal ego will, at times, defend the importance of the rejecting object (as the maintenance of the internal relationship is precious), and once again the analyst may have to pull back and wait for another opportunity to point out the reality of the rejecting object's indifference or maliciousness. During the narrative, the patient's central ego will "hear" some of the analyst's views and will slowly understand how hopelessly damaged the rejecting object really was and is. In Chapter Three, the importance of each of the part-self and part-object structures to each other was emphasized. Here the analyst disrupts the relationship between the antilibidinal ego and rejecting object by introducing split-off aspects of the rejecting object to the central ego, making this object worse than the patient ever imagined by stripping it of prestige and dignity. That is, the patient has avoided understanding that his parent was using the children to vent his/her frustration about his/her own childhoods or frustration about his/her place in the world. The true pathology of the parent is never fully understood by the angry, resentful but still admiring antilibidinal ego. The reality of the rejecting object is avoided by the antilibidinal ego simply because it firmly needs to believe that by displaying his/her goodness and arguing with the rejecting object, they will be able to change the rejecting object's mind. This is the point that Odgen made in the previous chapter, that the individual is dealing with objects that he/she has partially created, as opposed to the real objects. The startling statement by Kopp from Chapter 2, that his mother hated him and that his father did not care to intervene, is the goal of this approach is to destroy the illusions that the antilibidinal has about the validity of the rejecting object.

Over time, the integration of more and more split-off material that is released from the patient's unconscious is accumulated in the central ego because the patient has an alternative good object upon whom they can shift their dependency needs, and therefore no longer has to depend on their original objects. This allows them to give up hiding from his/her past, and the painful but significant information that has been dissociated. Over time, the impact of a new view of the parent(s) will undermine the libidinal ego, as well as the antilibidinal ego, as the central ego's newly constructed conscious view of the parent(s) will disallow the libidinal ego to hold on to fantasies that there is potential love hidden in their objects. The central ego's recognition that the parent was a deficient, hapless or malicious human being who was incapable of loving anyone overrides and disallows any libidinal ego fantasy. Thus, once a single structure is undermined, the whole inner world along with its structures collapses. This specific strategy of disrupting the relationship between the antilibidinal ego and the rejecting object was not developed by Fairbairn, nor by other writers in the field, and is unique to my approach to using his model.

An Example of a Clinical Narrative

The following example is a facsimile of an interaction that I had with a patient who was at that time 50 years old and had consulted me for her anger and dissatisfaction with the men in her life who she felt had all used her selfishly. The patient was a university administrator who was divorced and the mother of two adult children. In this dialogue, I used the word "exciting" to refer to a new man in her life, and I did so not to inform her of Fairbairn's model (which I never did except in the most vague and general way) but rather because it captured her emotional state when meeting a new man. Her style of psychopathology was similar to the histrionic personality disorder (Celani, 1976, 2001) with male objects being first seen as exciting objects, and then after they make an inevitable misstep, are suddenly split and then seen as rejecting. My patient had been raised in Europe and was basically abandoned by her father, who was away very frequently to be with a second family in a nearby country that he used to visit while on "business" trips. This reality was only discovered after his passing. The narrative (which, again, is a condensed facsimile) reveals that I was focusing on my patient's pursuit of one bad object after another with no recognition on her part of her role in the scenario. I have used this example previously (Celani, 2010:137–138).

Pt: I met a Broadway actor who is up here for a semester teaching at the University, and agreed to visit him in his apartment tonight.

Th: Well, you really seem to be jumping into things in a big way. Is this fellow more or less exciting than the man that you brought home from the office last week?

Pt: (Laughs) That Larry fellow is a real loser. I know what you are going to say about this sudden change, but this is how I really feel.

Th: Oh, I do not doubt for a moment that this change is how you really feel. I am reminded of how you used to wait for your father to come home. Didn't you tell me how you would dress up in your roller-skating tights and greet him on the driveway with a new trick that you had worked on when he got home? And didn't you throw the Christmas gifts that he gave you into the woods when he failed to come home? Wasn't that a sudden change of feeling as well?

Pt: I can't remember how this business is supposed to fit together. I really don't know if it has anything to do with today.

Th: Let me see if I can help you out. You actually had two fathers, an exciting one who filled you with hope and expectation and an unreliable one who let you down time and again. When you were waiting for the exciting one to come home you couldn't remember his unreliable side. Your actor friend is the new version of the exciting side of your dad, and you can't see any other possibility. Larry, your exciting friend from our last session, is now equal to the unreliable side of your father, and you are not able to see any good in him.

Pt: I really hope that this isn't right. I hate to think that I am so simple.

This is a historical interpretation that attempts to link the past to the present, and as you can see it wasn't accepted. It was too early in the treatment process, too wordy and too heavy-handed for this patient to accept. Bromberg (1998) has commented on the importance of a strong alliance between the participants for the patient to accept what he/she hears from the analyst.

> At the moment the patient is looking at himself through the analyst's eyes, he is also looking at the analyst in a very personal way. The ability of the patient to accept the image of himself that the analyst is offering is directly influenced by his ability to trust his perception of the person presenting it. So his rejection of the interpretation is not only a rejection of a view of himself, but also a rejection of an unpalatable view of the analyst – a view in which he experiences the analyst as asking him to substitute, without sufficient negotiation, the analyst's subjectivity for his own.
>
> (Bromberg, 1998:250)

Clearly, the patient to whom I made the interpretation was rejecting my view of her family and her enactments as I was not internalized as a good object who she would allow to modify her sense of herself; however, over time and gentle repetition of the aforementioned historical pattern, she was able to accept and internalize this vision of her development.

Interpretation in Fairbairn's model (after the analyst's subjectivity has been accepted by the patient) involves linking the patient's adult patterns of relating to others to their internalized patterns developed in childhood and repeated endlessly. Once the analyst finds the specific incidents of trauma, dissociation and enactment, the narrative carries on throughout treatment and becomes more sophisticated and detailed as the same issues and events are discussed again and again. The following passage from Davies and Frawley (1991) illustrates this strategy.

> As with all analytic work, it is ultimately the analyst's ability to both participate and interpret the unfolding historical drama and to relate this history to current interpersonal difficulties that encourages the progression of insight, integration and change. . . . Our belief is that the interpretive process within the analytic experience is the only way to end the dissociation, projection, projective identification, and reintroduction that makes the history of abuse not only a painful memory, but an ongoing reality. . . . Included in our conceptualization of the transformational aspects of treatment are the patient's experience of the analyst's availability and constancy, the analyst's willingness to participate in the shifting transference-countertransference reenactments, and finally, his or her capacity to maintain appropriate boundaries and set necessary limits.
>
> (Davies and Frawley, 1991:30–31)

One of my focuses in treatment was to emphasize the external transference, which involved discussing the patient's relationships with objects in the external world (Celani, 1993). This focus would inform the patient of the probable motivations of people he/she interacted with and offer them insights as to how dependency needs, aggression and use of splitting manifested in external objects, either within their family or peer group. Using this approach, the patient would become psychologically minded, which informed them of their own inner processes. It also avoids the direct impact of attempting to alter the patient's view of themselves, because it focuses on external objects and tends to arouse less resistance. Over time it helps to develop a stronger central ego in the patient and allows them to converse in a language shared with the analyst, as well as aids in the process of self-acceptance.

Working With Patients Who Contain Toxic Dissociated Truths About Their Childhoods

It is not always possible to develop a robust relationship with a patient before unconscious material emerges due to the pressure from the dissociated structures. My patient Angie (Celani, 2010) was such an example. She was raised in a large farm family where the children were sent to work outdoors on difficult tasks, often on tasks that were far beyond their capabilities. During her childhood, two of her brothers were severely injured in farm accidents. Angie was also assigned work far beyond her capabilities, including driving a large flat-bed farm truck loaded with logs, feed or hay to the family-owned farm store before she was tall enough to reach the pedals with her feet. She was born a fraternal twin and her brother was born severely mentally handicapped. Her mother blamed Angie for her twin brother's disability and punished her for trivial or non-existent reasons as much as possible. To avoid being punished, Angie spent much of her childhood playing in the barns until one of her older brothers went in the house and she followed him for protection from her mother. As an adult, Angie unconsciously found very difficult jobs in male-dominated industries and bitterly complained about her situation. She married and proved to be a difficult wife as she was hyper-active, often holding second jobs and indifferent to her husband's affection. She did display one unusual behavior, which was her extreme affection and concern about two shelter dogs she had adopted. When she came home from work, she would get on the floor and play and hug them, often tearing up. Her husband often complained that he wished that she would treat him as well as she treated her dogs. The marriage continued to deteriorate, and Angie's husband announced that he was going to ask for a divorce unless she sought treatment. This is typically a poor way to obtain a consultation, but Angie was not wary and proved to be an extremely lively patient who seemed relieved to have someone to hear her story.

We began about two months before Thanksgiving and I used my normal alliance with her central ego, as well as with her antilibidinal ego when it was the dominant structure, to comment on her developmental history, which was very poor at best. She was raised without love, exploited as a farmhand and excessively punished by her enraged mother. Despite this, her parents, who were very successful and owned three farms, declared themselves superior parents surrounded by grateful children, a vision that the children could not contradict. The now-adult children celebrated Thanksgiving at the family homestead, and each child brought a cooked dish to take the burden of cooking the whole dinner off their mother. Angie came to her session the week before Thanksgiving sobbing and almost unable to walk. I helped her into her chair and asked if she had been in an auto accident on the way to my office. She was unable to speak for a number of minutes and finally blurted out that she had had an awful dream. The dream was that she was required to kill, butcher and cook her two adored dogs as her contribution to the Thanksgiving dinner. The dissociated material in her unconscious about her mistreatment in the family was portrayed by her unconscious as a slaughter of innocence, which indeed it was. My strategy at this point was to quietly support her vision to not allow this key material to be dissociated again, and note how I saw hints in this reality during our narrative reconstruction of her history.

I cite the next patient because she displayed all the hallmarks of Fairbairn's mode, from dependency on her bad-object parents, to being attracted to bad objects and finally to enacting her internal structures in the external world. She came for a consultation in the early 1990s, and I presented this case to the 1996 Fairbairn Conference in New York City. My patient was a 55-year-old divorced woman with two adult sons who came in with a conflict based on her son's banishment from her parents' home. Her son had been invited to stay with his grandparents in Maryland for the summer as he was in between his junior and senior year of college, and he was asked to help his grandfather run his successful furniture business. However, during the first week, this young man discovered truths about his grandparents that upset him to distraction. His grandfather showed him how to use the switchboard, as he had three different retail stores. He was then instructed to distract and misinform his grandmother as to his grandfather's whereabouts by saying he was in the upholstery shop, on a delivery or in a sales meeting with a large customer. In actuality, his grandfather told him that he had a number of women he had seen frequently for many years, and during those times when he was visiting them he was unavailable. Interestingly, my patient confirmed that when she was a teenager, she had been recruited by her father to answer the switchboard and misdirect her mother as to her father's whereabouts, as were her two brothers who were also in on the scheme. The next task assigned to the grandson was to go to the liquor store to pick up the weekly supply of bourbon which he was instructed to drop off in a back room of one of the warehouses in a secluded gaming room where his grandfather and his golf buddies played cards and drank twice weekly. In the evenings, my patient's innocent and idealistic son witnessed a recurring verbal brawl between his grandmother and her 45-year-old son (his uncle), who lived in a basement apartment. His grandmother, who was also a heavy drinker, went down to her son's apartment to insist that he come up and have dinner and visit with his newly arrived nephew. The son, my patient's younger brother, had never left home; he worked for a landscaper and spent much of his time online. There was loud shouting, but the uncle never appeared for dinner. This pattern continued for ten days or so until the grandson could no longer tolerate the situation. He tearfully confronted his grandparents at dinner in regard to their drinking, his grandfather's womanizing and his grandmother's abuse of her dependent son. The grandparents froze, and his grandfather announced that he was to leave the next morning and was no longer welcome in their house.

This was the source of my patient's conflict, as her family was having a wedding party for their older son (my patient's other brother), who was getting married for the second time, and it was going to include family and friends. As I had learned of my patient's history of emotional deprivation from my detailed inquiry of her childhood, it seemed unlikely that she would be able to stay away, despite her desire to support her son by not going to the family party. Not unexpectedly, my patient chose to attend the party and had switched to her libidinal ego, eager to feel the love that she was sure was awaiting her. Once in Maryland, her libidinal ego dominated her perceptions, and she was thrilled to feel love all around her. During the party she decided to call me and berate me for "convincing" her that her family was dysfunctional. In fact, I would remind all of my patients of separate antilibidinal memories that did not fit into their litany of antilibidinal complaints about their objects, thus making them "worse" than the antilibidinal ego wanted to accept. During our sessions, she had revealed dissociated material to me (and to her central ego) that did not fit in with the isolated "truth" of her libidinal ego, which, despite the new information, now dominated her perceptions of her family. She assumed that she was alone in the house, as the party was in a tent in the backyard, and angrily picked up the phone to call me. At that moment, she was suddenly assaulted from behind by a person who was both hugging her and squeezing her breasts. She screamed and pushed the man down, then she recognized him – he was one of her father's golfing friends with whom she had had an affair when home from college some 30 years before. Despite the fact that this man was now in his eighties, he was able to get up and came at her again, but she picked up a dining room chair and threw it into his way, which terminated the attack. That night, after the party, the family was cleaning up and her mother went downstairs and loudly berated her brother for not joining the party.

These two incidents jolted my patient back into her central ego, and she remarked that she saw things very differently after they had occurred. Within two weeks of returning from Maryland, she described an incident that involved her son, who was now living with her for the summer, and a man with whom she had recently had an affair. She was driving down the main street of her town and saw this man and stopped her car and began a heated exchange with him. Her son jumped out of the car, pushed the man against the wall of a building and threatened to kill him if he ever talked to his mother again. This opened a whole new chapter in the treatment, as I had never been told anything about this affair. My patient, who had an administrative position in a medium-sized company, had been wooed by this 38-year-old man, who was a contract painter doing work inside the plant. He managed to stop at her office every time he was working and flattered her, saying how beautiful she was and how he wanted to date her. She finally agreed, despite their age and educational differences, and he showed up for the date with flowers and six bottles of champagne in the back seat. They went out for dinner and afterwards went to a motel and engaged in satisfying sex. This began a pattern of dating with one important variation – which was that my patient was physically abused during most of their dates. A pattern became established, which was after they had been drinking and had finished their first round of sex, her boyfriend would become suspicious, thinking that she had other relationships, and would tie her up and slap her. This would infuriate my patient and she would try to fight back as much as she could. As time would pass, he would feel contrite, apologize profusely and they would resume their sexual behavior.

This pattern of illusory love followed by abuse fit her inner structures perfectly. Her libidinal ego was in the thrall of her partner's (the exciting object) flattery, displays of affection and protestations of love. After he would become suspicious, he would become a vicious rejecting object, and she would switch to her antilibidinal ego and hate him with all the dissociated hate from her childhood. Her partner allowed her to tap into both of her powerful internal structures, her enraged antilibidinal ego and her love-obsessed libidinal ego. The separate, and opposite, "truths" that she was expressing were contained in the two isolated substructures. Each part-ego would emerge in turn and the antilibidinal ego would hate the rejecting object with complete abandon, and almost immediately, it would be replaced with her libidinal ego and express the need for love with equal intensity. My patient's alternating substructures were powerfully attracted to the opposite aspects of her object; her antilibidinal ego was intent on fighting with and reforming the rejecting object and her libidinal ego was intent on extracting love from the exciting object, and they required a partner who was able to rapidly switch from love to hate. This pattern, common in abused women (Celani, 1994, 1998) is an enactment of Fairbairn's key concept of "Attachment to Bad Objects". Mitchell's quote from Chapter 4 noting that the patient is not a passive container of bad objects, but rather actively seeks bad objects in the environment, is boldly illustrated in the behavior of my patient.

My work with this patient consisted of gradually introducing her central ego to the many aspects of parental failure that she had experienced and dissociated. She was deeply influenced by her internal structures, and her central ego was greatly attenuated. Over time, she gave up her attachments to exciting/rejecting objects and began dating an age-appropriate man who had no overly exciting nor overly rejecting behaviors. It would be difficult to understand this patient without the structural theory proposed by Fairbairn. It allows a psychoanalytic approach to reach a population of patients usually dealt with by public mental health institutions, if at all. When using Fairbairn's model, the analyst is equipped with an effective model which can help patients with painful histories to live a better life.

My last example is rather colorful, as it involved a patient who was unexpectedly trapped by her parents and used aspects of her treatment to gain her freedom. My patient was a very bright and exuberant Italian woman who came in for help separating from her overwhelming and controlling parents. She came to treatment with endless complaints about her parents, who constantly demanded that she return to their home because she was single (recently divorced) and therefore should remain with the family until she remarried, as tradition dictated. Her married brother was "required" to return home to his parents' house every weekend with his wife and child, and thus remained undifferentiated well into adulthood. My patient lived three hours away and was a very successful real estate broker and simply refused to comply, but was plagued by guilt.

When my patient entered treatment she saw her parents as benign, though excessively strict, and herself as a rebellious adult. That is, she credited her parents as having high standards that were based on family traditions. As we explored her history, I began to disrupt their "prestige" by pointing out that they were acting on their own behalf and using their children to protect themselves from a society in which they felt uncomfortable and overwhelmed. By binding their children to them, they avoided the larger world and focused on their children and grandchildren. These concepts were familiar to her, but she had pushed them aside and preferred seeing her parents from her libidinal ego. Her father was dramatic and bombastic, and this allowed me to approach this patient by undermining this aspect of his "prestige" that she still maintained in her antilibidinal ego. She felt guilty about not coming home, because she believed that her father was fundamentally correct. During our sessions I would role play his speeches about "family tradition" that my patient had described, and my patient would immediately start to smile knowingly. I would then participate in co-creating the narrative by interspersing the many ways that he had undermined his children's differentiation from "the family". I exaggerated and added humor to these clearly pathological behaviors that I added to my imitation of his speeches on "family traditions", which my patient's central ego accepted over time. It was a fun exercise and together we both recognized how emotionally disabled her parents were, and how much pain they had inflicted on their children by restricting them from experiencing life from their own subjectivity.

My patient's married sister had recently given birth to a daughter and had called my patient and invited her down to see the new baby, promising that she would not tell their parents. My patient agreed to visit her sister secretly and drove down one evening. She had a wonderful time visiting with her sister and playing with the new infant. As she was leaving her sister's house, her parents, who had been hiding in an unused room, jumped out and blocked her path, demanding to know why she had deserted the family! My patient was aghast, realizing that her sister had betrayed her, and now her parents were blocking her way out. She thought back to our role playing and apologized to her parents profusely, and dramatically praised "traditional values", just as I had in our sessions. The more she praised their values (and indirectly her parents) the more excited and relaxed they became. They all embraced and my patient promised to visit every weekend from then on. She ran out to her car and drove speedily back to Vermont and never returned to visit.

Fairbairn's metapsychology allows the analytic clinician to diagnose and treat patients who were once out of the range of classical analysis, with a seldom used analytic model that has to all appearances fallen into the history of psychoanalysis. Fairbairn's model was never seen as a viable treatment option; however, his model, when reconsidered in terms of modern metaphors and concepts, is a vitally useful and powerful treatment modality that can be used with a wide variety of patients.

References

Bromberg, P. (1998). *Standing in the Spaces*. New York: Psychology Press.

Celani, D.P. (1976). An interpersonal approach to hysteria. *American Journal of Psychiatry*, 113 (12): 1414–1418.

Celani, D.P. (1993). *The Treatment of the Borderline Patient: Applying Fairbairn's Object Relations Theory in the Clinical Setting*. Madison, CT: International Universities Press.

Celani, D.P. (1994). *The Illusion of Love: Why the Battered Woman Returns to Her Abuser*. New York, NY: Columbia Universities Press.

Celani, D.P. (1998). Structural sources of resistance in battered women. In Skolnick, N.J. and Scharff, D.E. Eds., *Fairbairn, Then and Now*. Hillsdale, NJ: Jason Aronson, 1998, pp. 235–254.

Celani, D.P. (2001). Working with Fairbairn's ego structures. *Contemporary Psychoanalysis*, 37: 391–416.

Celani, D.P. (2010). *Fairbairn's Object Relations Theory in the Clinical Setting*. New York, NY: Columbia Universities Press.

Davies, J.M. (1998). Repression and dissociation in Freud and Janet: Fairbairn's new model of unconscious processes. In Skolnick, N.J. and Scharff, D.E. Eds., *Fairbairn Then and Now*. Hillsdale, NJ: Jason Aronson, pp. 53–69.

Davies, J.M. and Frawley, M.G. (1991). Dissociative processes and transference-countertransference paradigms in the psychoanalytically oriented treatment of adult survivors of childhood sexual abuse. *Psychoanalytic Dialogues*, 2 (1): 5–36.

Fairbairn, W.R.D. (1943). The repression and return of bad objects (with special references to the "war neuroses"). In *Psychoanalytic Studies of the Personality*. London: Routledge & Kegan Paul, 1952, pp. 59–81.

Schafer, R. (1992). *Retelling a Life: Narration and Dialogue in Psychoanalysis*. New York: Basic Books.

Schafer, R. (1996). Authority, evidence, and knowledge in the psychoanalytic relationship. In Renick, O. Ed., *Knowledge and Authority in the Psychoanalytic Relationship*. Northvale, NJ: Jason Aronson, 1998, pp. 227–244.

Searles, H. (1958). The schizophrenic's vulnerability to the therapist's unconscious processes. In Searles, H.F. Ed., *Collected Papers on Schizophrenia and Related Subjects*. New York: International Universities Press, 1965.

Skolnick, N.J. (2014). The analyst as a good object: A Fairbairnian perspective. In Clarke, G. and Scharff, D.E. Eds., *Fairbairn and the Object Relations Tradition*. London: Karnac, pp. 249–262.

Index

Printed in the United States
by Baker & Taylor Publisher Services